Social Identity in Question

D0141392

Social identity theory is one of the most influential approaches to identity, group processes, intergroup relations and social change. This book draws on Lacanian psychoanalysis and Lacanian social theorists to investigate and rework the predominant concepts in the social identity framework.

Social Identity in Question begins by reviewing the ways in which the social identity tradition has previously been critiqued by social psychologists who view human relations as conditioned by historical context, culture and language. The author offers an alternative perspective, based upon psychoanalytic notions of subjectivity. The chapters go on to develop these discussions, and they cover topics such as:

* self-categorization theory;
* group attachment and conformity;
* the minimal group paradigm;
* intergroup conflict, social change and resistance.

Each chapter seeks to disrupt the image of the subject as rational and unitary, and to question whether human relations are predictable. This is a book which will be of great interest to lecturers, researchers and students in critical psychology, social psychology, social sciences and cultural studies.

Parisa Dashtipour currently teaches in the School of Social Sciences at Cardiff University.

Concepts for Critical Psychology: Disciplinary Boundaries Re-Thought

Series editor: Ian Parker
Manchester Metropolitan University

Developments inside psychology that question the history of the discipline and the way it functions in society have led many psychologists to look outside the discipline for new ideas. This series draws on cutting-edge critiques from just outside psychology in order to complement and question critical arguments emerging inside. The authors provide new perspectives on subjectivity from disciplinary debates and cultural phenomena adjacent to traditional studies of the individual.

The books in the series are useful for advanced-level undergraduate and postgraduate students, researchers and lecturers in psychology and other related disciplines, such as cultural studies, geography, literary theory, philosophy, psychotherapy, social work and sociology.

Forthcoming Titles:

Cultural Ecstasies
Drugs, Gender and the Social Imaginary
By Ilana Mountian

Social Identity in Question
Construction, Subjectivity and Critique
By Parisa Dashtipour

Self Research
The Intersection of Therapy and Research
By Ian Law

Social Identity in Question

Construction, subjectivity and critique

Parisa Dashtipour

Routledge
Taylor & Francis Group

LONDON AND NEW YORK

First published 2012
by Routledge
27 Church Road, Hove, East Sussex BN3 2FA

Simultaneously published in the USA and Canada
by Routledge
711 Third Avenue, New York NY 10017

Routledge is an imprint of the Taylor & Francis Group, an informa business

© 2012 Psychology Press

British Library Cataloguing in Publication Data
A catalogue record for this book is available from the British Library

Library of Congress Cataloging-in-Publication Data
Dashtipour, Parisa.
Social identity in question : construction, subjectivity, and critique /
Parisa Dashtipour. -- 1st ed.
p. cm.
Includes bibliographical references and index.
ISBN 978-1-84872-080-0 (hardback) --
ISBN 978-1-84872-081-7 (pbk.)
1. Group identity. 2. Interpersonal relations. 3. Social change. I. Title.
HM753.D37 2012
305--dc23
2012003784

ISBN13: 978-1-84872-080-0 (hbk)
ISBN13: 978-1-84872-081-7 (pbk)
ISBN13: 978-0-203-10358-6 (ebk)

Typeset in Times
by Integra Software Services Pvt. Ltd, Pondicherry, India

MIX
Paper from
responsible sources
FSC
www.fsc.org   FSC® C004839

Printed and bound in Great Britain by
TJ International Ltd, Padstow, Cornwall

For Cyrus

Contents

Preface

Psychology as a discipline reflects a number of popular assumptions about the nature of the 'individual' as locus of action (the site of perception, cognition and motivation) and the 'social' as the mere context in which individuals view and make sense of the world, and feel impelled to either take part in it or hide themselves away from it. Critical psychology questions the assumption that there must be a split between those two sides of the equation, and this book homes in on the subfield of 'social psychology' that always promises alternatives to the dualism of its host discipline but again and again fails to deliver. This book goes right to the heart of one of the most ambitious attempts from within laboratory-experimental social psychology to provide a genuinely social account of identity, that of 'social identity theory', and finds it wanting.

Parisa Dashtipour engages in a sympathetic and rigorous reading of social identity theory – hers is the best critical insider account we could wish for – and is able to show us exactly how and why it fails to escape the individual–social dualism of its host discipline, psychology. And then she goes further, to explore the 'discursive' tradition in qualitative research that seemed to fill the gaps left open by the social identity theorists. Again, she takes the most radical accounts of discourse in social psychology, and shows us through a careful analysis of the theoretical claims in that tradition that there is still something missing.

This is where psychoanalysis comes into play, specifically the work of Lacan and his followers, and here Dashtipour leads us into the domain of fantasy and conflict, and some clear case examples to make the point. The social identity and discursive paradigms, she tells us, both fail to offer a satisfactory answer as to why social categories can have such influence on its members. Lacanian psychoanalysis now underpins her argument that, in addition, those social psychological theories are unable to adequately account for the subjective complexities involved in resistance and change. Having thrown social identity into question, then, we move into an innovative account of 'construction, subjectivity and critique'. *Social Identity in Question: Construction, Subjectivity and Critique* thus begins with a detailed analysis of theories in social psychology, but by the end of the book we have resources from psychoanalysis that sidestep dualism in psychology, and we have a new way of thinking about the relationship between the 'inside' of the individual and the social world 'outside' them. To take psychoanalysis seriously as a line of work often excluded from mainstream psychology also enables us to move into a completely different realm 'outwith' psychology altogether.

Ian Parker
Discourse Unit
Manchester Metropolitan University

Acknowledgement

I should like to thank Professor Ian Parker for his support in completing this book, and Dr Derek Hook for his contribution to a previous version of the book.

1 Introduction

In social psychology and other related disciplines, social identity theory (SIT) is among the most influential theories of group processes and group-induced change. It was developed more than a few decades ago, challenging the way groups were previously understood and generating a serious interest in group issues. Some argue that the SIT tradition[1] has been particularly prominent in its theorization of the individual–social relation in the discipline (Brown & Lunt, 2002). The SIT approach is perceived as original in a discipline where theories are becoming increasingly 'micro', and its influence has strengthened in recent years (Hornsey, 2008). Part of the reason for this is that it views collective issues, such as social influence, not as effects of intra-personal or inter-personal processes but as part of larger-scale social dynamics. The paradigm takes seriously status differences and power struggles between groups and emphasizes that subordinated groups are able to criticize and propose alternatives to the prevailing social order. It has been characterized as a theory that is primarily focused on social transformation because it illustrates how social identities change, and how categorization is involved in collective action (Reicher, 2004; Tajfel, 1981).

A focus on the SIT approach is important because it motivates reflection on the nature of conformity, power and resistance – issues that critical psychologists are deeply interested in. Critical psychology aims to criticize inequalities and injustices in the world, and it is acutely concerned with social change. It is equally preoccupied with assessing and challenging mainstream psychological theories. This book is therefore dedicated to investigate, question and reinterpret one of the most dominant traditions in social psychology. The SIT paradigm is a broad field, and it is applied to a variety of topics. One area of social life, which contemporary social identity researchers do not sufficiently explore, is social change (Reicher & Hopkins, 2001a). Chapters 6–8 in this book concentrate therefore on the part of the theory that focuses on resistance, collective struggle and change.

Given that extensive reviews of the social identity paradigm can be found elsewhere (e.g. Brown, 2000; Hogg & Abrams, 1988; Hornsey, 2008; Reicher, Spears, & Haslam, 2010; Tajfel, 1978, 1981, 1982; Tajfel & Turner, 1986; Turner & Giles, 1981), only a brief sketch is provided below, and Chapters 3–6 will open up and scrutinize some aspects of the theory in more detail. The final part of the present chapter offers an overview of the main arguments of this book. Before we move on, however, it should be made clear that this book will largely centre on the original texts of SIT and self-categorization theory (SCT) (as they were presented in, e.g. Hogg & Abrams, 1988; Tajfel, 1978, 1981, 1982; Tajfel & Turner, 1986; Turner, Hogg, Oakes, Reicher, & Wetherell, 1987).

Social identity theory: a motivational and socio-cognitive account of intergroup relations and social change

Tajfel and colleagues developed SIT while a debate had already taken root about the reductionist and individualistic trends in social psychology. The theory emerged as a critique of accounts that depicted prejudice as an effect of intra-psychic frustration or authoritarian personalities (e.g. Adorno, Fenkel-Brunswik, Levinson, & Stanford, 1950; Dollard, Doob, Miller, Mowrer, & Sears, 1939). One of the main postulates of SIT is that prejudice and conflict are predominantly related to group membership rather than, for example, individual aggression, or even scarce resources as believed by Sherif, Harvey, White, Hood, and Sherif (1961).

SIT was initially built to account for the findings of the famous experiments known as the 'minimal group paradigm' (Billig & Tajfel, 1973; Tajfel, 1970; Tajfel, Billig, Bundy, & Flament, 1971). In these experiments, participants were divided randomly, or on the basis of trivial criteria (e.g. preference for Klee or Kandinsky paintings) into two groups. There were no prior interactions between the participants, no knowledge of who was in the ingroup and outgroup. The subjects only knew which group they belonged to and they were given the task of allocating points to other participants. The results of these experiments suggested that subjects allocated maximum rewards to the ingroup in manners that increased the difference between the amount allocated to the ingroup and to the outgroup (the minimal group experiments will be discussed in more detail in Chapter 5). Tajfel concluded that this finding must be related to the subjects' sense of belonging to the groups in which they had been allocated. The change from personal to social identity leads to a shift from interpersonal to intergroup behaviour. Since there was no interpersonal contact, no history and no common goals between members of the groups, the researchers deduced that knowledge of group membership is sufficient for the creation of a sense of group belonging and for positive differentiation (ingroup favouritism). In other words, beyond any historical, economic and political factors, simply belonging to a group is a sufficient condition for the development of ingroup favouritism. The minimal group experiments resulted in the explanation of prejudice in terms of social categorization, social comparison and group membership (see Tajfel, 1978).

Social categorization is "the ordering of social environment in terms of groupings of persons in a manner which makes sense to the individual" (Tajfel, 1978, p. 61). It is a meaningful process, related to the individual's system of beliefs, and it works as a guide for action; it helps one to orient oneself in society. The idea of categorization is largely derived from Tajfel and Wilkes' (1963) earlier research on the accentuation effect: a cognitive consequence of categorization that leads to stereotyping. It is human nature to try to understand the physical and social environment and thus categorization, which simplifies the complex world, is a means through which people can make sense of this complexity. Social categorization exaggerates differences between groups and minimizes differences within groups. "Social categorization per se induces the perception of intragroup similarities and intergroup differences" (Turner, 1981, p. 79). Social categories are evaluated positively or negatively, and this process helps to enhance differences between and similarities within categories. Tajfel (1978) argues that the "interaction between socially derived value differentials on the one hand and the cognitive 'mechanics' of categorization on the other is particularly important in all social divisions between 'us' and 'them'" (p. 62). The interplay between cognition and social structure is thus seen as significant; as well as a cognitive process, categorization is a "socially evolved representation of social structure" (Turner, 1996, p. 20). Categorization changes the way people see themselves and each other, it makes salient 'us' and 'them' differentiations, which leads to intergroup discrimination: "Social categorization ... seems to be the effective cause of intergroup discrimination" (Turner, 1981, p. 78). It is, however, acknowledged that something else has to be involved in discrimination or negative prejudice. There must also exist a motivational aspect to discrimination.

SIT implies that our social identities are constructed by the numerous social categories we identify with. These are not all activated simultaneously. Rather, our social identity depends on the social category made salient in specific contexts. Salient social categories define the self and the social context and lead to a process of social comparison that in turn leads to self-evaluation (Tajfel & Turner, 1986). Turner argues that

> the categorization process produces the perceptual accentuation of
> intragroup similarities and intergroup differences and thus makes salient

or perceptually prominent the criteria or relevant aspects of ingroup–outgroup membership. In this way, it selects the specific dimensions for self-evaluation and social comparison in the given setting.

Turner (1981, p. 82)

Group belonging is important as a basis for self-definition. Individuals therefore search for positive ingroup distinctiveness, and discriminate against other groups. This produces competitive intergroup relations. In other words, our membership categories have significant implications for our self-esteem so there is a strong motive to positively evaluate social identity. People compare their own group with other groups in order to "create, achieve, preserve or defend a positive conception of oneself, a satisfactory self-image" (Tajfel, 1981, p. 338).

Social comparison is an idea borrowed from Festinger (1954) who believed that man is characterized by "a drive to evaluate his opinions and his abilities" (p. 117) and this occurs through comparison with others, especially with those others who are superior to him. Tajfel (1981) states: "a group becomes a group in the sense of being perceived as having common characteristics or a common fate mainly because other groups are present in the environment" (p. 258). The attributes of a group gain their importance in comparison to other groups, and the values attached to the differences between groups are significant in this process. "The definition of a group (national, racial or any other) makes no sense unless there are other groups around" (Tajfel, 1978, p. 66). Turner argues that intergroup comparisons are related to the status differentials between groups in society:

> status differences represent the outcomes of intergroup comparisons conferring positive or negative distinctiveness and also the antecedent conditions for different social strategies ... directed at the maintenance or protection of self-esteem.

(Turner, 1981, p. 81)

Those who belong to groups that are generally perceived to be 'inferior' can resist this representation of their group and gain a more satisfactory sense of self by positively distinguishing their group from other groups. Reicher (2004) emphasizes that the social identity approach allows for flexibility, creativity, innovation and agency. He points out that social change or collective movements fundamentally depend on the way identities are constructed and renegotiated. "What the social identity perspective offers, then, is an understanding of how shifts in categorization come about and how they are related to collective action" (Reicher, 2004, p. 941). He also states that minority members' group actions are "aimed at challenging and dismantling current structures of inequality rather than creating and defending them" (p. 932). However, subordinated groups very often simply accept their group membership and its 'inferior' evaluation. With the exception of a limited number of cases (e.g. Hinkle & Brown, 1990; Moscovici & Paicheler, 1978; see also Chapter 15 in Tajfel, 1981) this problem has largely been neglected in the SIT paradigm. Investigating the underlying reasons for this acceptance is crucial because not challenging a denigrated group evaluation inhibits social change and generates immense psychological and social costs (Augoustinos & Walker, 1995).

SIT points out that instead of identifying with the dominant group and thereby accepting an inferior position, members can act in order to change their status (e.g. Tajfel, 1981; Tajfel & Turner, 1986; Turner & Brown, 1978). The theory focuses on "what explains this new behavior whereby status systems that kept subordinate groups 'in their place' for years are now under attack" (Turner & Brown, 1978, p. 202). It is this aspect of the theory that has inspired Billig (2002) to argue that it is essentially "a theory of group freedom", and that "the most original parts of the theory describe how groups can recreate stereotypes that are applied to them" (p. 179).

In order to reconstruct stereotypes or escape a stigmatized social identity, various resistance strategies could be applied depending on subjective belief structures. When the boundaries of social categories are seen as permeable, people employ an individual strategy and distance themselves from – or exit – the negative social category. They no longer define themselves in terms of this category and will try to gain acknowledgement in the dominant group – this is called the social mobility belief system. For example, this kind of strategy may be used by some people with an immigration background in European countries: they can change their names into Western sounding names, in order to 'pass' as a member of the majority group because they believe it will be easier for them to gain access to jobs and other privileges that come with belonging to the majority group. However, this could be seen as an assimilation strategy (Tajfel, 1981), or even as 'identification with the outgroup' because the ingroup is discriminated against and the outgroup favoured. Individual mobility does not have any influence on the overall structures of inequality and the status quo will be maintained.

The social change belief system is based on the assumption that group boundaries are impermeable, and that the status of the denigrated minority group can be changed (Tajfel & Turner, 1986). Whether or not subordinated groups will engage in various forms of collective action depends, however, on the existence of 'cognitive alternatives'. This is when the subordinated group perceives the social system as illegitimate and changeable. When cognitive alternatives exist, one group of strategies that minorities can employ is 'social creativity', which may entail the following: The negatively evaluated groups can introduce new dimensions through which they can compare themselves against other groups in more positive terms. Alternatively, they can change the value of those aspects that are considered inferior and reverse these. Another strategy involves comparing with other 'low-status' groups rather than with the dominant group. If subordinated groups apply any of the above consistently, they may bring about a change in the way they are perceived, and attain a positive social identity. A more radical social change strategy labelled 'social competition' by Turner & Brown (1978), includes the struggle for more profound changes, for example, by engaging in demonstrations, wars or terrorist acts in order to gain the recognition and respect which the affected groups feel they deserve. Social competition involves the idea that recognition is not something that is simply awarded by those in power to those who are disempowered but is something that must be taken, even if by aggressive, violent means, if it is in fact to be worthwhile.

In order to discriminate against other groups and/or engage in collective action, individuals first need to view themselves as part of a group. How are social identities and social categories made salient, and how do people identify with a group? The issues of group membership and group influence are tackled by SCT.

Self-categorization theory: a socio-cognitive account of the group

SIT shows that social categorization is the foundation for psychological group formation: people demonstrate shared responses according to the ingroup. Imposing a shared group membership on subjects seems to be enough for people to like each other and to act in accordance with each other, and discriminate against other groups. SCT (Turner, 1985; Turner et al., 1987) develops this major conclusion of SIT. SCT illustrates how subjects are able to act in terms of a group as a result of social identity, which is "a higher order level of abstraction in the perception of self and others" (Turner et al., 1987, p. 42). A psychological group is formed when people define themselves in terms of shared ingroup categorization. This theory moves away from the focus on intergroup relations and investigates group processes in general, and the ways in which the group and its norms and values become significant for individuals. In other words, it deals with the consequences of groups on individual members. It is specifically dedicated to a rereading of traditional theories of social influence. The questions addressed in SCT are, for example,

How does a collection of individuals become a social and psychological group? How do they come to perceive and define themselves and act as a single unit, feeling, thinking and self-aware as a collective entity? What effects does shared group membership have on their social relations and behavior?

(Turner et al., 1987, p. 1)

There is a return here to categorization processes with an emphasis that one's self-perception is significant in the formation of groups. While SIT could be understood to include some motivational elements, SCT is primarily a cognitive branch of the SIT paradigm.

Self-categorization applies to three general levels; there are three different levels of belonging: superordinate (being part of humanity), intermediate (group membership) and subordinate (individual self-definitions). The claim here is that groups that have psychological importance are based on a shared sense of identity. This sense of identity is founded on the perception of oneself as an interchangeable member of the group, rather than a distinct individual. When a category is salient, people categorize themselves into that group. Group membership or social categories have important psychological and behavioural consequences for the group member. Group membership itself can be understood "as a distinctive explanatory process in social psychology" (Turner et al., 1987, p. 1), and various social phenomena such as social influence, collective behaviour and attributions are directly or indirectly caused by people's knowledge of being part of a group (see Turner, 1991, 2005; Turner et al., 1987).

Two notions explaining the salience of categories are 'accessibility' and 'fit'. These terms are based on Bruner (1957) who claimed that the activation of categories produces a perception of reality that to a large extent reflects that reality. Fit and accessibility show the significant impact of context on categorization. A category becomes salient when it is readily accessible and can become activated, and when an actual stimulus fits the stored category specifications in a given situation. The accessibility of a category depends on past experiences and current goals and purposes. Perceivers are thus actively selective in their use of relevant categories. 'Comparative fit' refers to the idea that a given categorization becomes salient when differences within categories are less than differences between categories; when intergroup rather than intragroup differences are noticeable. This idea is related to earlier work on categorization (see above), but SCT develops it by demonstrating that this process is dynamic and determined by context and situational factors. 'Normative fit' means that the fit between category and reality depends on the expected content dimension; salient social categories and the stereotypes associated with them depend on the social meaning, the content, of the observed situation. Self-categorization theorists argue that fit "ties perception firmly to reality" (Oakes, Haslam, & Turner, 1994, p. 116).

The presumption that categorization is a cognitive distortion of the world is thus rejected:

> given the reality of groups and individual's identifications with them, there would be conditions under which groups-based perception (of both the self and others) would be entirely appropriate (and not a dysfunctional oversimplification and distortion of the uniqueness of individuals).
>
> (Oakes, 1987, p. 141)

SCT claims that people generally represent their social group in terms of prototypes and when a social category becomes salient they see themselves less as individuals and more as prototypical examples of the group. Hence, "categorization of self and others ... accentuates the group prototypicality, stereotypicality or normativeness of people" (Hogg & McGarty, 1990, p. 13). It is important for group members to have their attitudes confirmed by the relevant social category. Social facts depend on their confirmation by significant group members (Turner et al., 1987). The more an individual is similar to ingroup members and unlike outgroup members, the more that individual is assumed to be prototypical of the ingroup. Members are popular and socially attractive when they appear to strongly conform to group prototypicality (Hogg & Hardie, 1991).

Seeing oneself as a group member rather than a separate individual leads to depersonalization, which

> refers to the process of 'self-stereotyping' whereby people come to perceive themselves more as the interchangeable exemplars of a social category than as unique personalities defined by their individual differences from others.
>
> (Turner et al., 1987, p. 50)

Depersonalization is thus "a change from the personal to the social level of identity [and] the functioning of self-perception at a more inclusive level of abstraction" (ibid, p. 51). We define ourselves and our actions according to the characteristics that define our group. We conform to the group stereotype as we stereotype ourselves. Depersonalization is at the basis of group cohesion, social influence processes, shared norms, co-operation, collective behaviour, altruism, social stereotypes and ethnocentrism (Turner et al., 1987).

Moving beyond current critiques of the social identity paradigm

Some recent social identity research emphasizes the historical and cultural context, and the flexible and fluid nature of category use (see in particular the discursively orientated social identity research by Reicher, 2004; Reicher &

Hopkins, 1996). Reicher (2004) does not view categorization simply as a function of cognition or perception but a process of changing or maintaining certain structures of power and making possible collective action. He promotes the theory as an illustration of power and resistance. Furthermore, it is now more common to argue that legitimacy of a group's social position is a more reliable cause of ingroup bias than individual self-esteem (Hornsey, 2008). More recently there has been a renewed interest in the motivational causes of group processes and intergroup behaviour, but motivation for distinctiveness and self-definition, rather than self-esteem, is now seen as crucial. Instead of construing comparison and self-esteem as an individual process, Reicher (2004) points out that social comparison is carried out at group level and the self-esteem hypothesis should be understood as the evaluation of the ingroup category. Some argue that the need for social meaning and guidance on what to think and how to behave causes much group behaviour, and group distinctiveness is crucial in offering such guidelines (Hogg, 2000). Despite the important recent developments, social psychologists have challenged the theory for a variety of reasons, and many researchers prefer alternative perspectives on social identity and social change, such as those offered by discursive psychology.

Chapter 2 will review these criticisms and discuss the alternative discursive approaches. One of the main claims of this book is that such developments may be important, but neglecting the psyche and the affective dimension means ignoring significant aspects of group processes and social change. For example, Billig (2002) argues that motivation should not be reduced to individual motivation for self-esteem. This is because motivation is a fundamental factor in extreme forms of prejudice, and he aspires to reintroduce certain elements of intergroup hatred which SIT aims to dismiss: "bigotry seems to include the very psychological components that the cognitive approach sought to exclude ... these are emotional or motivational factors, adding an intensity and willfulness to mere categorical exaggerations" (Billig, 2002, p. 178). He therefore reintroduces the issue of emotional investment in prejudice and categorization processes, but his claim is that these emotions should be understood as "constituted within social, discursive interaction" and "need not be seen as an individual condition, located within the body of the individual" (Billig, 2002, p. 179). It has already been noted by some researchers in social psychology that extreme forms of intergroup hatred, such as that involved in bigotry and prejudice, cannot simply be defined as a discursive process, because they entail intense non-discursive, bodily and affective elements (e.g. Frosh, 2002; Hook, 2005, 2006, 2007). The present book moves beyond recent challenges to, and rereadings of the SIT paradigm (such as those offered by Billig, 2002). In Chapter 2, the discursive perspective is criticized for often ending up reproducing an image of the subject as coherent and voluntary, and for depicting social categories as largely a matter of discourse and knowledge. Even when this perspective does highlight the ambivalent and contradictory nature of subjectivity, it simply states that ambivalence and contradiction exist; not much explanation of such phenomena is given. For example, ambivalence may arise not only because social categorization and social change strategies are complicated discursive actions but also because they involve the operation of desire, a desire that is fundamentally the desire of the Other. More than just this, group membership, such as being part of a nation, and social change efforts, such as social competition acts, involve not only cognitive and discursive processes, but also bodily experiences, which cannot be reduced to the cognitive or the discursive. Although it is absolutely necessary to investigate each intergroup relation separately, those analyses which do not take this non-discursive, non-cognitive factor into account, are often inadequate because they ignore the way people passionately invest in categories, and they do not sufficiently elaborate on the ambivalence of resistance and social change acts.

The social identity tradition has offered an understanding of the processes that may be involved in groups and intergroup relations. It may have been important in the explanation of the *how* of group effects, intergroup behaviour and resistance. Discursive psychology, with its focus on wider cultural processes, may have evoked a focus on *why* certain categories rather than others are used in specific circumstances. However, SIT and the discursive paradigms both fail to offer a satisfactory answer as to *why social categories can have such influence on its members*, nor do they adequately account for the subjective complexities involved in resistance and change. Both approaches are unsuccessful in answering certain significant questions, such as:

- How can we explain the passionate or zealous nature of intergroup differentiation or prejudice?
- What is it that underlies the motivation to seek positive distinctiveness?
- In whose gaze is distinctiveness desired?
- Why do groups have such important consequences for individuals?
- Why do people conform to group norms?
- Why is there sometimes a resistance to change identities?
- Why do social movements and revolutions often result in a new form of subordination?

An understanding of the 'psychological' or the 'psyche' is required for an adequate explanation, even if we end up with a very different notion of the 'psychological' to the one presumed in mainstream forms of social psychology (see Parker, 2003). We need to identify "the different levels at which identification matters" (Stavrakakis, 2008, p. 1053), and cannot be satisfied staying at the cognitive, social or discursive levels. By making recourse to the theory of Jacques Lacan – in particular to those authors who have shown how Lacan can be used in social analysis (such as Alcorn, 2002; Bracher, 1993; Glynos, 2001, 2003; Glynos & Stavrakakis, 2008; Hook, 2008a; Pavón Cuéllar, 2010; Stavrakakis, 2007, 2008; Žižek, 1989, 1993, 2006, 2008) – it is possible to open up and rethink the main postulates of the social identity paradigm, and point to significant factors of social identity and social change that are fatally under-theorized. This book proposes that a reinterpretation of the social identity tradition needs to move beyond a discursive reworking and include an understanding of desire, and the affective component of socio-political life.

Turner et al. (1987) argue that "logically speaking, [SCT] is more general and can be seen to include [SIT] as a derivation" (p. 43). Therefore, after a review of the critiques of the SIT paradigm in Chapter 2, this book begins its Lacanian reinterpretation with SCT in Chapter 3. In this chapter, some of the predominant concepts of Lacan are introduced. Let us acknowledge here that simplified versions of Lacan's ideas are often applied in this book. This makes sense since his philosophy is exceedingly obscure and complicated. Every attempt has been made, however, to do justice to his theory. It should also be stressed that the use of Lacanian psychoanalysis is very limited here. The aim is not to offer an alternative Lacanian theory of groups and intergroup relations. Rather, it is to bring in concepts in order to challenge and rework the main ideas in the SIT tradition. The present book therefore only makes use of those Lacanian notions that contribute to an elaboration and critique of the SIT approach. In Chapter 3, for example, the 'psychological group' is translated into the 'symbolic Other', and the 'prototype' is compared with Lacan's notion of the 'ego-ideal'. The main argument of Chapter 3 is that SCT confuses the difference between self-categorization and categorization by the socio-symbolic field of the Other. Self-categorization is a fiction, an imaginary construction, while our identification with (or alienation in) the discourses of our group is what produces us as subjects. The category (as understood in terms of the signifier), rather than the 'self', should then be deemed as primary in intragroup processes.

Chapter 4 continues to focus mostly on SCT in order to highlight some neglected elements of the group process such as recognition and love. It discusses ways to consider the affective nature of group attachment. This is the physicality, the 'hot' aspects, of the group bond not sufficiently theorized by SCT or the discourse analytical approach. By affective, we mean libidinal economy: a certain kind of bodily experience linked to enjoyment. This chapter also shows how differentiation should be viewed in terms of enjoyment: it is a matter of preserving the distinctive ways in which a group gains its enjoyment. Furthermore, the paradox of the group bond is pointed out in this chapter. For example, why is it that the practice of mocking or parodying the ideals of a group rarely ends up seriously subverting these ideals? It is perhaps not surprising that the rationalistic tradition of SIT completely disregards the fact that the breach of official group demands can, oddly enough, function to strengthen group solidarity.

Chapter 5 applies some of the Lacanian concepts introduced in Chapters 3 and 4 to reread the minimal group experiments. It is suggested here that these experiments and their results should be understood as a function of the language (or discourse) of the experimenter. The experimenter introduces in the experimental setting group differentiations using signifiers that participants can identify with or against. In this sense, the experiments illustrate very well the symbolic effects on subjectivity. They are good examples of the way language transforms and determines subjects. The significance of this chapter should be viewed against a theoretical and methodological background in social psychology where the role and the influence of the experimenter in determining results are completely ignored or brushed over.

Chapters 6–8 mainly focus on an examination and elaboration of the social change aspects of the SIT approach. Chapter 6 begins by arguing that the 'social mobility' belief system in fact constitutes a fantasy. It is this fantasy that sustains the belief in social mobility, and works to loosen the cohesiveness of subordinated groups and inhibits collective action. The chapter then moves on to problematize the prediction that the existence of 'cognitive alternatives' would lead to collective struggle. People may know at a cognitive level that change is possible, but they may still invest, libidinally, in their symbolic position. Indeed, when taking libidinal economy and desire seriously, we can begin to see the ambivalence that characterizes many collective actions. The chapter follows SIT in claiming that social groups are not divided or structured equally. Some groups in society have more power over desire and identity than others. What we can deduce from this is that, in social creativity, not any arbitrary set of attributes, not all potentially available group images, can function as the basis of a satisfactory identity. The Lacanian notion of the 'desire of the Other' is used to reinterpret social creativity strategies. It is thus the big Other that authorizes what would be a 'positive' identity. The chapter is also a critique of many discursive perspectives that focus on the discursive renegotiation of categories and disregard the role that desire may play in the process. In light of these discussions, Chapter 6 asks whether SIT's 'social change' strategies would be better understood as socio-symbolic symptoms.

Chapter 7 uses the Swedish anti-racist magazine *Gringo* to offer a more 'empirical' illustration of some of the points made in Chapter 6 and some other parts of the book. We will see here how social creativity is related to desire, and how there can be a libidinal investment in the image of 'difference'. The chapter will show how and why the 'search for distinctiveness' is heavily affectively loaded. A secondary function of this chapter is to suggest some ways Lacanian theory could contribute to methodological processes in social psychology, particularly to the analysis of textual or discursive material. The book concludes in Chapter 8 by emphasizing that a viable social change 'belief structure' is less a matter of cognitive transformation than affective change. More specifically, collective action often follows a change in desire, and this change is most progressive when it involves a modification in the organization of subordinate groups' enjoyment.

Why Lacanian psychoanalytic theory?

The SIT approach was developed as a critique of previous theories of prejudice that made use of psychoanalysis. The latter "must at all costs be kept outside the social identity tradition, since it threatens to disrupt the rational model of the individual which lies at its core" (Brown & Lunt, 2002, p. 8). This is one of the most important reasons why there is an urgent need to bring back psychoanalytic concepts: to dismantle the image of the subject as rational, transparent, conscious, coherent and unitary. This reflects a broader "need to change social psychology so as to open it to Lacanian psychoanalysis" (Pavón Cuéllar, 2010, p. xv). For these reasons, the terms 'subject', 'subjective' or 'subjectivity' are applied very differently in this book to the ways the SIT paradigm may use them. Subjectivity refers in the present book to the condition of being a human being within a material and socio-discursive context (see also Henriques et al., 1984, p. 3). It alludes to the psychoanalytic notion of the subject as constituted by desire and language. The Lacanian notion of the 'symbolic' already takes seriously the fact that each subject is produced by a broader socio-historical context. The benefit of this approach is, therefore, not only that it "avoids positing a positively defined essence of subjectivity" but also the fact that it "moves beyond psychological reductionism and individualism" (Stavrakakis, 2008, p. 1041). A more complicated perspective on subjectivity and identity is needed not least because Tajfel (1981) attempted to avoid their complexity: he did not want to "enter into endless and often sterile discussions as to what is identity" (p. 255). A discussion about the intricate nature of identity is nevertheless significant because identity is not just some abstract philosophical notion, but as SIT researchers very well recognize, it is absolutely pertinent in social processes and social change. Once the complexity and intricacy of identity and subjectivity are taken seriously, many of the conclusions of the SIT tradition become questionable. Let us emphasize here that rather than identity, a Lacanian perspective would stress identification as a continuous process of subjectivity. In psychoanalysis "subjectivity becomes the space where a whole 'politics' of *identification* takes place" (Stavrakakis, 2008, p. 1041). Lacanian theory is thus urgently needed in social psychology because, as Bracher states,

> it offers a comprehensive model of the human subject that includes ... the fullest account available of the various roles that language and discourse play in the psychic economy and thereby in human affairs in general.
>
> (Bracher, 1993, p. 12)

Of course Lacan and social psychology are not exactly compatible (see Parker, 2003). Concepts from SIT would sit very uncomfortably with those from Lacanian psychoanalysis. Indeed, Lacan's "insistence on the primacy of the signifier over the subject – and his commitment to analyses of the functioning of the unconscious structured like a language – precludes any easy assimilation into orthodox psychological thought" (Hook, 2008a, p. 67). However, psychology has a "historical tie to psychoanalytic concepts", and we would therefore do well to "show how deeply indebted psychology is to genuinely psychoanalytic concepts" (Parker, 2000, p. 334). To be sure, "Lacanian theory offers important insights into many of what we might consider the constituting problematics of social psychology" (Hook, 2008a, p. 52). Rather than rejecting SIT and promoting in its place a Lacanian approach to group and intergroup processes, this book therefore attempts to pick dominant ideas from the SIT framework and demonstrate how they compare with a psychoanalytic perspective. An outright dismissal of the SIT tradition would be ineffective since, as we know from psychoanalysis, that which is suppressed tends to keep reappearing, and sometimes with even greater force. Analysis is better than dismissal because critique all too often structurally depends on that which has been dismissed.

Let us emphasize that this book aims less at final explanation, or a universal theory of groups, and more at disruption. It is ironic that Tajfel, the founding father of an approach that explains group and intergroup processes, was uncomfortable with theories that set themselves out to 'explain' or 'explain away' social phenomena, especially horrific phenomena such as the holocaust (Billig, 1996). Lacanian theory questions whether anything can *ever* be explained. This is because explanations never manage to cover everything, there will always be something left unexplained. That does not mean that we should stop being curious or asking questions about identity, groups and intergroup relations. The objective here is to analyse and thereby disrupt mainstream psychology's often taken for granted faith in the SIT tradition and its image of the rational individual. Such a disruption is urgent given the powerful presence of this tradition in many undergraduate courses, and given its influence in informing policy on, for example, ethnic relations in many Western countries.

Although it would be impossible to offer a universal theory of identity and intergroup processes, certain mechanisms of affection, for example, seem to reappear across cases of group and intergroup relations. For instance, one cannot fully understand British identity without closely studying how the British category has been produced, and able to gain significance, in a specific historical context of colonialism. In many respects, however, some aspects of identifying with Britishness are not too different to, for example, the way people may identify with the 'Greek' or 'Muslim' categories. One last note to be made here before we move on to the next chapter is that the book follows much of the SIT tradition in focusing on social categories that matter for people. These are often large-scale categories based on, for example, ethnicity, religion, class, political affiliations, and gender. This is not to say that some of the issues discussed cannot be applied to smaller-scale groups such as sports teams or corporations.

2 The social identity tradition and its critics

Henri Tajfel, the founding father of the social identity tradition, aimed to develop a non-reductionist social psychology that views the individual as embedded within a historical and socio-cultural context. He was suspicious of theories that characterize the human being as autonomous, and he believed that people's position within a material and political context and their subjection to a system of social norms and values condition their mind and action. He insisted that social psychology alone could not explain social phenomena. His thought "contains a number of intellectual similarities with the sort of social constructionism often seen to represent a very different type of social psychology than social identity theory" (Billig, 1996, p. 336). Despite Tajfel's ambitions for a new form of social psychology, the subsequent development of SIT has been heavily criticized for its reductionist understanding of social behaviour. This is partly a consequence of the ambiguities and contradictions that existed in Tajfel's own writings and work (Billig, 1996, 2002; Condor, 1996; Wetherell, 1996a). On the one hand, he wanted to develop a social psychology that seriously takes history, culture and the ideological context into account. On the other hand, he was dedicated to the experimental method and emphasized individual cognition and universal psychological processes.

This chapter reviews some of the main criticisms of the social identity paradigm. The various critiques of the theory are often interrelated, but they will be discussed here under the following separate headings:

- individualism, rationalism and universalism;
- psychological processes at the expense of content and meaning;
- the neglect of history, culture and context;
- the neglect of language and communication.

The discursive or social constructionist perspective in social psychology offers another approach to social identity, categorization and change. This approach is discussed in this chapter and some of its limitations are outlined. The chapter ends by introducing Lacan's notion of the symbolic and the signifier as alternative ways to understand cognition and categorization.

Individualism, rationalism and universalism

Despite Tajfel's aim to move social psychology away from a focus on the individual, the SIT tradition's emphasis on individual cognition, and its implicit (or explicit) individual–social dichotomy, have been heavily criticized. "Social identity theory has become a search for an explanation in individual and psychological (social cognitive) terms" (Wetherell, 1996a, p. 279). Cognitive explanations are reductionist as they reduce the complex socio-cultural and historical nature of groups and intergroup relations into processes of individual cognition (see Farr, 1996). Wetherell and Potter (1992) take issue with this paradigm where individuals are seen as "self-contained and independent organisms, with perceptual systems, distinct cognitions and motive systems" (p. 46). Within the SIT tradition, individuals are "endowed with such natural powers as the ability to categorize sense data into meaningful ideational units" (Brown & Lunt, 2002, p. 6). Contextual and social issues are seen as external to the individual, existing merely as a set of stimuli to which the individual responds. SCT in particular tends to break the world down into separate levels and variables for use in experimental manipulation and statistical analysis (Condor, 2003), and relations between groups are thought to exist as a series of outside stimuli that are cognitively processed within the individual mind. For example, "maleness, masculinity, gender differences are all described as a 'set of relations being represented'. They constitute the input to a representational process occurring within the individual" (Brown & Lunt, 2002, p. 9).

The SIT paradigm also problematically views social life as a function of cause-and-effect sequences where the rational motives of the individual are brought to the fore. In particular, changes in the social environment, such as processes of globalization that are outside the control of the individual or the singular group, are overlooked and "far too much weight is given to the role of the rational individual in producing change" (Brown & Lunt, 2002, p. 10). Researchers within the SIT framework often assume that the stability or disruption of the social system reflects belief systems and activities *intended* to maintain or change the social order. Social action, however, often has unintended and unexpected consequences:

> Social identity theorists often come close to espousing voluntaristic and teleological models of history and social change which neglect the ironic character of human social activity: the fact that in the ongoing

process of translation over time and dispersal over space, our actions may come to have (or at least, contribute to) consequences that we never anticipated.

(Condor, 1996, p. 293)

Reicher (1996) claims that social action can come *before* belief structures, perceptions of legitimacy and cognitive alternatives, instead of the other way around. He argues that very rarely do revolutionary movements start with an alternative vision of society. "It is only through their actions, the retaliations of those in power or else their impotence in the face of mass actions, that the existing regimes are delegitimized and possible futures are glimpsed" (p. 325).

The universalistic assumptions that underlie the SIT paradigm are also strongly challenged. Although some of Tajfel's writings cautioned against universal psychological explanations and 'truth claims', "social identity theory is a universal theory, both in terms of its key concepts and its core assumptions about individual motivations" (Billig, 1996, p. 346). Researchers in the SIT approach are not very interested in historical differences and tend to focus on the similarities between cases of intergroup behaviour. Emphasizing common characteristics while disregarding differences is problematic. Can we treat all categories as if they were the same? Do, for example, national and professional categories function in the same way? In the SIT tradition, "psychological processes are abstracted from their historical contexts in order to be treated as instances of generalities" (Billig, 1996, p. 347). Billig finds it problematic to, for example, describe the Nazi holocaust in terms of the Germans' search for positive distinctiveness. The universalistic assumptions of categorization in the SIT paradigm also imply that prejudice is inevitable (Augoustinos & Reynolds, 2001; Wetherell & Potter, 1992). The focus on categorization as a universal process directs attention away from the fact that apart from categorizing and simplifying, people are also capable of particularizing the social world (Billig, 1985). Wetherell's (1982) research challenges the idea that there is one universal process of intergroup conflict. Minimal group experiments in cultures that emphasize generosity do not demonstrate the same level of discrimination. Her study with Maori and Pacific Island children showed that they do not discriminate to the same extent as British and North American children. This implies that each intergroup behaviour needs to be understood within a particular social and cultural framework. There is no automatic relation between categorization and discrimination. Wetherell states that

what may be more crucial is the way in which group members interpret and give meaning to the intergroup situation in line with their collective frameworks of their culture and community. This sense making will determine the consequences of group identification – whether it leads to in-group favoritism and out-group discrimination or to some other outcome.

(Wetherell, 1996b, p. 218)

Reicher and Hopkins (2001b) make it clear, however, that differentiation is not the same as discrimination. They state that from a SIT perspective "differentiation occurs on *valued dimensions of comparison*" (p. 34). It therefore becomes possible that in certain cultures groups can differentiate by being more charitable than other groups. Acknowledging this nonetheless requires paying attention to the broader system of values and meanings in a given society.

Psychological processes at the expense of content and meaning

The SIT paradigm's emphasis on psychological processes at the expense of meaning has been challenged (Duveen, 2001; Huddy, 2001; Verkuyten, 2005). Duveen (2001), for example, believes that although Tajfel was very much concerned with what it *meant* to be defined as a Jew in Europe in the 1930s or a black in Britain in the 1970s, the subsequent research in the SIT approach tends to focus on "processes through which identity is sustained or manipulated rather than on the content of those identities" (p. 259). Duveen's position is that social categories are meaningful and they tend to impose themselves on individuals: identity includes a process of "being identified" (p. 259). A significant problem with the SIT tradition is that "it offers a theory of the consequences of categorization, but is mute on the question of why individuals should categorize themselves in particular ways" (p. 268). People already belong to wider systems of representations or categorizations that predate any individual. We allocate ourselves within those categories that have already located us. Howarth (2002) criticizes the SIT approach for its "emphasis on how we categorise ourselves, and its relative inattention to how others categorise us … categorisation may in fact be imposed on one" (p. 158). She also argues that because of the experimental foundation of the theory "the lived realities of the dialectic of identity have been simplified" (p. 157).

The emphasis on group boundaries in SIT is at the expense of the meaning of group membership (Huddy, 2001). The boundaries of certain social identities are also more vague than is assumed by the SIT tradition. It becomes, for example, difficult to theorize the complex and negotiated 'in-between', hybrid categories such as Black-British identities from the perspective of the SIT tradition (Verkuyten, 2005). Indeed, categories and group boundaries are not already 'out there', but very often negotiated. Reicher and Hopkins (1996) state that it is problematic to assume that categories can be read from social reality. In the SIT approach

> social reality [is] taken as a given for the perceiver who will then be treated as akin to a cognitive automaton which internally computes categories from the objective array of stimuli ... The frame of reference cannot be taken as self-evident.
>
> (Reicher & Hopkins, 1996, p. 355)

The view of categories as already given, and the problems of individualism and universalism are partly an effect of the SIT tradition's tendency to ignore the historical, cultural and the contextual nature of identities and intergroup relations.

The neglect of history, culture and context

SIT research is often criticized for neglecting historical, cultural and contextual factors, and disregarding the specificity of social identities and intergroup relations. Meaningful categories are acquired over time through cultural ideologies specific to a context. The experimental foundation of the theory does not allow for an adequate understanding of real-world groups that are a result of complex socio-historical and political processes. Social identity theorists who employ the experimental method tend to bracket out the dynamic nature of real-world social phenomena, construct a static and reified nature of intergroup behaviour, and overlook "the ways in which intra- or intergroup processes may unfold and transform over time" (Condor, 1996, p. 292). Reicher (1996) argues that social identity research obsessed with the experimental method tends to view social life as motionless, and neglects Tajfel's original ideas on social categories as contextually and historically bounded guides for social action.

Wetherell (1996a) implies, however, that this may be due to the ambiguous nature of Tajfel's writings: on the one hand he viewed human behaviour as conditioned by historical and cultural norms and values, so the social and the individual cannot be viewed as separate entities. On the other hand, he believed that basic individual psychological processes exist that are separate to socio-cultural and historical factors; social norms and values are merely 'content' that fills out the universal psychological processes. Wetherell regrets that Tajfel's initial explanations of the minimal group results were abandoned in favour of explanations that emphasize cognitive universal laws (see also Condor, 2003). In one of the early papers the results of a minimal group study were explained in terms of "a 'generic' social norm of ingroup–outgroup behaviour which guided the [subjects'] choices ... the norm of 'groupness' may be expected to operate when the social world of an individual (at least in our societies) clearly dichotomized into 'us' and 'them'" (Tajfel et al., 1971, pp. 174–175). Wetherell (1996a) states that what the subjects bring to the experiments, their prior knowledge of social conduct, is emphasized in this account. This way of viewing intergroup behaviour as a product of wider social and cultural norms and values was unfortunately lost in the later development of SIT. Tajfel's attention was drawn "away from the social and ideological context towards the 'general psychological processes' thought to interact with ... social context" (Wetherell, 1996a, p. 280).

Brown and Lunt (2002) discuss how the social identity approach has, in recent years, become even more experimental, which is absurd for a theory that aims to explain prejudice – a phenomenon that essentially reflects complex, historically grounded and politically motivated relations between groups. They argue that in order to circumvent this problem, researchers in the SIT tradition frequently invoke Tajfel's personal experience as a Jewish immigrant from Nazi Germany. Brown and Lunt call this strategy 'the Tajfel effect'. It "can serve to designate a particular kind of interaction between the theoretical, experimental and biographical elements of a tradition of research which operates to prevent the tradition becoming disconnected from the phenomenon which it purports to explain" (p. 5). The more the findings of SIT experiments become stripped off from reality, "the more pressing [is] the need to repeat Tajfel's settlement" (p. 7).

Brown and Lunt (2002) strongly challenge the fundamental assumptions of the SIT tradition. They argue that the cognitive or perceptual powers of the individual only function within a broader social and material setting that gives them meaning. They particularly criticize the way SIT research attempts to theorize the individual–society relationship: "What is... problematic in the way social identity theory relates the individual to society is the artificial separation of individual rational agents from wider processes of power and representation" (p. 9). The argument here is that individuals are involved in social practices that already give meaning to categories before individuals can begin to think about them. Individuals therefore draw upon and participate in *existing* forms of descriptions and categorizations. Categorization is then not a cognitive but a collective process that involves a multiplicity of meanings. The authors emphasize that we therefore need to "reconsider the complexity of the links between social identity and social structure" (p. 19). The broader *infrastructure* in which categories or groups operate should not be overlooked in our studies of identity and intergroup relations.

When the broader infrastructure is taken into account, self-categorization researchers' characterization of identity and categorization as flexible and situational becomes less convincing. This characterization reflects a narrow understanding of 'context' as the local, immediate situation (in the laboratory experiment), rather than the broader social and longstanding ideological myths and images that make up a particular culture (Condor, 2003). This issue of the degree of flexibility of identities has, however, received contradictory criticisms. On the one hand, some commentators view identities as considerably stable and not as fluid and flexible as those created in the laboratory of SIT research. Condor (1996) argues that SCT in particular "leaves us with the problem of accounting for (or even conceiving of) continuity *over* time" (p. 289). Strong identities in the real world are not so affected by the immediate situation. Huddy (2001) states, it is "difficult to believe that a group prototype can be changed as easily as suggested by self-categorization researchers" (p. 148). On the other hand, the SIT approach is challenged by Brown and Lunt (2002) for depicting identity as *too stable*: "social identities have greater degree of mutability than social identity theory is prepared to allow", social categories are "always up for renegotiation not only in groups, but whatever the setting happens to be" (p. 10). Moreover, Wetherell (1996b) states "the process of identification ... seems to be more flexible and moment-to-moment than social identity theory ... implies" (p. 222).

These seemingly contradictory responses may be due to the fact that within the SIT tradition, stability and flexibility are both eminent. Society is on the one hand seen to consist of clear-cut, stable and coherent categories, an idea which is actually a "subtle adoption of a form of Marxist social theory" (Brown & Lunt, 2002, p. 10). The actions of powerful groups will reproduce their status, stabilize a stratified social system and inhibit change (Tajfel, 1981). On the other hand, "the question of flexibility and context-contingency of subjectivity has ... been emphasized by researchers adopting Turner's self-categorization approach" (Condor, 1996, p. 288). It is nevertheless, as Condor states "possible to overstate the extent to which people in contemporary societies regard identities as voluntary or transient" (p. 304). She discusses the ways in which categories are often subjectively experienced as endurable and continuous rather than modifiable. Social action is usually future orientated and reproduces identities (or categories) across time. Identities are also perceived as a generational phenomenon that "transcends mortality" (p. 306). Indeed, social identities are sometimes fiercely protected for future generations:

> We experience a sense of stewardship over the 'heritage' of the social
> groups to which we belong, and see it as our duty to protect this heritage

for future generations, even if it is not clear why, or if, our successors might want it.

(Condor, 1996, p. 307)

Researchers within the SIT paradigm do not take these types of subjective experiences into account, even though they acknowledge that members often experience an imaginary sense of simultaneity or unity with the group. They are also silent on the issue of *how* this sense of unity can come about. It is often via communicative practices, through language, that geographically dispersed individuals can come to be unified within groups or categories. It is here that we will raise one very problematic shortcoming of the social identity tradition: the lack of a theory of language and communication.

The neglect of language and communication

Many social identity theorists and especially self-categorization researchers assume that members of geographically dispersed groups often act in a seemingly spontaneous and unitary manner. Condor (1996) claims that even if there were cases where geographically scattered people could come to act and feel in a unitary fashion, social identity theorists do not raise or address the issue of how this can come to be the case. In order to explain how people can in some circumstances come to act in similar ways, we need to take the issue of communication seriously. Social identity theorists have "generally been reluctant explicitly to enter 'communication' as a variable in their accounts" (Condor, 1996, p. 29). Indeed, the whole field of language has, since the beginning of the development of the theory, been a neglected topic. "For Tajfel, it is probably fair to say, language was not an issue" (Wetherell, 1996a, p. 280). Even if language was of interest, it was simply viewed a psychological rather than a socio-psychological matter.

Taking communication and language into account, we can come to accept that not all communicative messages will be taken up, or reacted to, in the same way. We can therefore assume that "any social identification is open to multiple interpretations", and not all individuals react to social identities such as 'Britishness' in the same way (Condor, 1996, p. 299; see also Brown, 1996; Huddy, 2001). Condor argues that researchers in the minimal group experiments constructed rather than 'found' uniform responses, because with the use of statistical manipulations they eliminated differences between individuals in the experiments. She further claims that communication technology, such as TV and the Internet, can in a very powerful way give individuals the opportunity to co-ordinate their actions. "In an important sense, then, the very phenomena which social identity theory attempts to explain (the behavior of people as members of spatially dispersed 'imaginary communities') are, themselves, the result not of universal sociopsychological processes, but of socio*technical* systems" (Condor, 1996, p. 302). Modern communication technology facilitates the production of group descriptions that people can come to identify with, and the proliferation of imagery that can mobilize large groups of people. These technologies cannot, however, by *themselves* explain how they manage to have this effect on people. Certain psychological processes must be involved that would allow for the powerful impact that certain group images – spread by these technologies – can have on individuals. This is why merely sociological or discursive accounts are often inadequate in the explanation of social identities and social mobilizations. The limitations of the discourse analytical perspective on identities and categorization will be discussed later in the chapter. The following offers a short overview of the discursive approach in social psychology, and a summary of the ways in which the discursive perspective has reworked some notions of the SIT paradigm.

The discursive approach as an alternative to the SIT paradigm

Some assumptions in the SIT perspective such as the comparative and the situational nature of identity, resemble poststructuralist ideas that flourished in the social sciences and humanities between the 1960s and 1980s (Condor, 1996). The lack of conceptual engagement with language in the SIT tradition has, however, been seen as problematic by poststructuralist or postmodern social psychologists who view language as constitutive of social life. These researchers have proposed the translation of cognitive processes into processes in language, as elements of discourse, which can be explored with theoretical and methodological tools from discourse analysis.

Discourse analysis has its roots in philosophy, sociology and literary theory (Potter & Wetherell, 1987). The discursive perspective is a vast and varied field. The different strands of the discursive approach are, however, united by their limited concern with the experimental method. They are also "united by a common attention to the significance and structuring effects of language, and are associated with interpretive and reflexive styles of analysis" (Burman & Parker, 1993, p. 4). Researchers in this field do not focus on processes within individual minds. They are rather interested in the ways in which language structures perception, and produces meanings that reflect wider social conditions. Crucially, "the focus is not on the individual *per se* but on the *forms of life* and the *activities* which make up sociality" (Wetherell, 1996c, p. 5).

Discourse is a general term that lays emphasis on linguistic practice. Discourse could be seen to consist of "all forms of spoken interaction, formal and informal, and written texts of all kinds" (Potter & Wetherell, 1987, p. 7). The discursive approach in psychology is part of a wider social constructionist perspective in the social sciences where "the relationship between what is 'inside' and 'outside' language [is] problematized" (Burman & Parker, p. 4). Generally speaking, a discourse is an institutional and ideological "system of statements which constructs an object" (Parker, 1992, p. 5).

The world as we perceive it, including the groups we belong to, and relations between our groups and other groups, are discursively and linguistically framed. Social constructionist approaches aim to "describe the constitution of the group and the individual, not to presuppose them" (Parker, 1997, p. 188). Discourse analysts do not generally look for something that lies beyond language – for example, 'real' cognitive states, attitudes or beliefs – but focus on discourse itself, the way it puts into practice pre-existing linguistic resources in order to construct a particular version of the world as opposed to another. An account not only portrays/describes something but also has an ideological and material function. The emphasis is on the *interactional* aspect of psychological phenomena, and the "'action orienta-tion' or 'function orientation' of discourse" (Gill, 1996, p. 142). The exam-ple provided by Eagleton (1991) demonstrates this principle of discourse analysis: "a pronouncement like 'black is beautiful' ... looks on the surface as though it is characterizing a state of affairs, but is in fact of course a rhetorical act of defiance and self-affirmation" (p. 19). Discourses are means of social practice that do things (e.g. blaming groups, defending oneself, repressing certain accounts). They also enable certain practices to happen (or not to happen); discourse has 'real' effects. Discourse is also a rhetorical act aimed to win over opposing positions or possible criticisms: "the emphasis on the rhetorical nature of texts directs our attention to the ways in which all discourse is organized to make itself persuasive" (Gill, 1996, p. 143). Researchers pay attention to the immediate interpretative context in which the discourse is being uttered, because it is largely the given situation that conditions meaning.

Some discourse analysts also carefully study the wider, ideological con-text. In critical discourse analysis (e.g. Fairclough, 1989, 1992) the focus is on the ways in which text and discourse work to reproduce power and inequalities. Social conflict and issues of stake are thus seen as fundamental aspects of social life. Discursive psychologists such as Wetherell (2004) (see also Augoustinos, Tuffin, & Rapley, 1999; Dixon & Durrheim, 2000; Dixon et al., 1994; Wetherell & Potter, 1992) emphasize how identity and inter-group relations are influenced by discourses in culture via internalized social dialogues. Such symbolic tools give us the building blocks of the cognitive and identity functions that provide the basis for many psychological operations; they supply the means through which we can make sense of events and ourselves. Identities, in this perspective, are a struggle over representation; they are effects of power: "power is closely linked to the *formation* of subjectivity, to the very making of identity" (Wetherell, 1996d, p. 314). Social identities are then both micro, and macro: they are a product of both local, contextual everyday negotiations, *and* of wider historical and political constraints. This perspective blurs the distinction between the personal and the cultural or collective, between what is 'personal' identity and what is 'social' identity. In talk and text, people take on meanings existing in culture, of what is 'the ideal' (e.g. the ideal self) and reproduce them (Wetherell, 2004). This leads to an important difference to the SIT tradition, which focuses mainly on process, namely the fact that now the content of identities is brought to the fore, and the wider cultural and ideological context are the starting point for any analysis of group identity and group relations. No universal process of human life and intergroup relations are implied, and the minimal group results are reinterpreted from a social constructionist perspective to claim that the wider cultural and social context will provide the tools with which people can make sense of the intergroup situation. This approach views description of groups as derived from ideologically structured narratives, dialogues and social practices.

Categories in language

We have stated that in the discursive perspective, the cognitive and perceptual processes described in the social identity tradition are understood as *activities* carried out in discourse and language. Rather than looking for categorization processes within people's minds, discourse analysts explore how verbal categorizations are complex modes of social accomplishments. Potter and Wetherell (1987), for example, investigate the work of categorization in everyday discourse and text, and the functions it serves in particular contexts. "Instead of being a victim of mechanical categorization processes people will both draw flexibly on preformed categories and construct the sense of categories as they talk" (p. 121). They focus on the ways people use or create categories in talk and text to *do* things, such as blaming, defending or justifying. There is thus an emphasis on the action orientation of categorization. Billig (2002) notes "categorization and stereotyping can be investigated within discursive interaction" (p. 184). In the discursive translation of categorization, the stress is put on the way group categories are used in practice and "how offensive descriptions of groups are embedded in arguments and in complex and shifting webs of categorizations" (Wetherell, 1996b, p. 220). According to Wetherell (1996a) the discursive perspective allows for the detailed and first-hand study of "power, the process of categorization, the creation of identity and movement for social change" (p. 282). Categorization itself is viewed as an effect of power and wider ideologies that both structure and change human relations. Categorizations therefore have immense political implications.

This view on categorization is very different to the one suggested by the SIT paradigm, especially the one proposed by the SCT. Categories are not seen as a given 'out there' in 'reality'. Moreover, discourse analysts do not impose preformed categories on research participants. Instead, they study how categories become relevant by investigating how they are produced through language and discourse, and how they become reified or 'naturalized' through rhetoric in a given situation. But "rather than categorizations being switched into activity by situations, discourse works to define events, and make relevant its situations, by the kinds of categorizations it deploys" (Edwards, 1998, p. 18). Discourse analysts are therefore not interested in the terms often used by experimental researchers such as 'perception', 'variables', or 'stimulus'. Further, "there is no explanatory primacy given to *self* categorizations, as a psychological starting point for how everyone sees the world" (Edwards, 1998, p. 17).

Categories are not used to explain various intra- and intergroup phenomena. Rather, categories are *constructed* via a discursive process of argumentation and debate. There are often disputes over the meaning of social reality as well as group membership, boundaries and categorizations. Reicher and Hopkins (2001a) insist that rather than social reality consisting of social categories, social categories *create* social reality. They are very critical of the ways social psychology in general, including self-categorization theorists, have focused on what happens to people's cognitions and behaviour given certain categories. Social psychologists have neglected the question of how categories and group divisions and identities come about. Even though the immediate context is taken seriously by SCT, the fact that both context and categories are created and reified through a rhetorical process is overlooked. Self-categorization researchers do not consider "how rhetoricians argue over identities even within a specific context and how they seek to render their own particular version as the sole authentic identity" (Reicher & Hopkins, 2001a, p. 397). Categories *are made* to seem part of the natural world. Certain category definitions are framed and 'naturalized' with the use of discursive rhetoric. This is a method of closing off alternative constructions and categorizations of the social world. The reification and naturalization of categories involves hiding the process of negotiation and concealing the contingent nature of categories (Reicher & Hopkins, 2001a). Despite acknowledging the ways categories stabilize identities and the social order, there is also a great deal of work that investigates and highlights the way categories and group descriptions are challenged and renegotiated.

Renegotiating categories and social realities

The discourse analytical field is largely focused on the argumentative and rhetorical character of discourse, and on the contested, hybrid and fluid nature of identity. There is therefore a particular focus on the possibility of changing social relations. Hopkins, Kahani-Hopkins and Reicher (2006) recognize that a focus on agency and social change should also acknowledge the issue of power limiting social change; they warn us to beware of the dangers of falling into a "pernicious voluntarism" (p. 54). They nevertheless claim that in a social psychological theory of social action, social relations and transformation "the concept of identity must be central [and] those marginalized and oppressed by particular identity definitions may reconstrue their collective identifications so as to realize social change" (Hopkins et al., 2006, p. 56). Much of the research within the discursive paradigm is thus concerned with the problem of how people disrupt certain forms of categorization and critically engage in identity construction and alternative discourses. Given that discourse constructs only one version of the social world, there is always a possibility for alternative descriptions; people can resist dominant modes of categorizations.

This perspective is then very much concerned with the motivations and interests of those who are doing the categorization work. If motivations and interests vary according to the person doing the categorization in a given context, it follows that categories also vary. "The variation and the active reconstruction of categories cannot be easily reconciled with the popular cognitive models" (Potter & Wetherell, 1987, p. 136). Rather than viewing categories as preformed permanent entities, researchers within the discursive perspective focus on the variability of category contents. Categories are seen as negotiated in specific localized contexts, in text and talk (Billig, 1997; Edwards, 1998; Wetherell & Potter, 1992). For example, Wetherell and Potter state

> the process of categorization, and thus the psychology of categorization, resides, not just in the mind, but we would suggest, within discourse as part of a collective domain of negotiation, debate, argumentative and ideological struggle.
>
> (Wetherell & Potter, 1992, p. 77)

Challenging the stigma attached to, for example, 'minority' identities is a process involving the discursive renegotiation of categories, traversing or contesting their content and value in specific contexts. Hopkins and Kahani-Hopkins (2004) (see also Hopkins, Reicher & Kahani-Hopkins, 2003) underline the significance of a discourse analytical approach in the understanding of contested, collective identities and political action. In their study on the Muslim community in Britain, they suggest that highlighting contestation, rhetoric and argumentation is crucial in order to counter the essentialist academic and popular notions of Islam where the "Muslim's agency [is] denied" (p. 353). They state "actors are able to transform their representation of themselves and their interests. That is, behavioral change ... is a product of changes in actor's social identifications and characterizations of their identity-related interests" (p. 354). In their view, "strategic construction of identity lies at the heart of constructing and communicating alternative characterizations of British Muslims' predicament" (ibid.).

Hylton and Miller (2004) similarly adopt a discursive perspective, but they use the narrative approach to argue that the social category of 'blackness' or black subjectivity can be interpreted in "terms of a change in narrative from a 'Tragic Negro' to 'Romantic Black' to 'Satirist African'" (p. 397). Thus, "the nature of identity is such that we are [the] constituent of the stories (accounts, discourses and language-games) in which we become animated" (p. 392). Identity is therefore viewed as constructed through available or appropriate stories, and as essentially historical, fluid, hybrid and relational. Their paper discusses the possibilities for a fluid black identity to shift radically after the 1960s. Duncan (2001) likewise examines the identities of black youth, and argues for a discursive understanding of the black identity which emphasizes the "competing discursive positions that shape their subjectivities in ways that are complex and contradictory even as they are partial and in flux" (p. 98). Along these lines, the author claims "the activities of racialized youth take on a global character to challenge disparaging myths, as evident, for instance, in the international appeal of hip-hop culture" (p. 99).

Another example is Kirkwood, Liu, and Weatherall (2005) who stress the significance in paying attention to the ways the white majority group in New Zealand resists discriminatory discourses about indigenous rights. They employ an argumentative or rhetorical analysis in order to investigate counter-hegemonic accounts "that may facilitate personal and political action against discrimination" (p. 502). Their position is that "engagement with opposing arguments is crucial for the development of critical thought" (p. 503). Likewise, Lynn and Lea (2003) point out the dialogic and intertextual nature of ideology, identity and critical thought. According to these authors this perspective "sees people as shaped by discursive practices, but also capable of shaping and therefore structuring those practices" (p. 431). They demonstrate how letters written by members of the public to British national newspapers construct the asylum seeker as the 'enemy', but at the same time they examine the rhetoric of a counter-discourse which positions the state's lack of democracy rather than the asylum seeker as the enemy.

They conclude that "only by frequent (re)exposure to this counter-discourse will commonsensical, taken-for-granted attitudes be challenged" (p. 448).

Reicher and Hopkins (1996, 2001a, 2001b) believe that social identities (or categories) are absolutely pertinent in the transformation of the world: "practice (in the sense of action that is organized in order to bring about certain transformations of the social world) would be impossible without social identity" (Reicher & Hopkins, 2001a, p. 399). In order to mobilize people and implement change, the use of social categories is often necessary. Identity categories define what is possible and not possible. They use SCT in their analysis of collective mobilizations, but they view salience and definitions of categories as determined in argument and discourse. Rhetorically and argumentatively defined group self-categories are significant in the speech of those who aim to mobilize masses. The definition of categories, their content and prototypicality tend to form collective mobilizations: "category constructs in political rhetoric reflect a speaker's project of mobilization" (Reicher & Hopkins, 1996, p. 369). Social categories do not therefore only maintain a specific social order; they are also used to create new ones. A historical dimension, the relation to time, is crucial to consider because categories "orient as much to the future as to the present" (Reicher & Hopkins, 2001a, p. 384). This is why it is important to focus on action, rather than perception. They view "social identities as models of one's place in a system of social relations along with the forms of action that are possible and proper given that place" (2001b, p. 398). The meaning of social identity is a matter of debate and negotiation, and people can change the world and create a new future by changing the definition of categories and contexts. Categories are then very much about "becoming" (Reicher & Hopkins, 2001a, p. 42). This implies that those who are interested in changing the world and shaping the future will have to renegotiate the meaning of categories; they have to become "entrepreneurs of identity" (ibid, p. 49). Discursive characterizations of events, people, and categories more generally, facilitate mass mobilization of people and social change.

The authors nevertheless acknowledge that there are limits to the extent in which people can reshape their categories and their reality. The structure of the social world will constrain the categories that can be used: "our models relate to our possibilities of action in the real world, and the categories that we use will reflect the constraints on how we are able to act" (Reicher & Hopkins, 2001a, p. 399). Categories and the extent to which they are able to change should be understood within a historical and interactive process. The effects of the actions of a given group depend to a very large extent on the ways their actions are understood and reacted to by others. For example, if a group of people are treated and seen as 'oppositional' by others, they will often come to see themselves as 'oppositionists'. The actions of a group can therefore have unintended consequences due to contextual changes and the ways they are being seen and defined by others. Their overarching argument is, however, that categories are the source of change, "they are bound up with our struggles to make and to move in the world" (ibid, p. 401). They state, for example, that subordinated groups' "use of social categories is a response to practices that subordinate them on the basis of that category membership, rather than because of any timeless essence to the category" (ibid, p. 402).

However, even if there is no timeless essence to categories, the discursive perspective fails to state *why people often assign a timeless quality to categories*. Reicher and Hopkins' translation of the social identity paradigm within the discursive perspective offers a very useful elaboration of social identities and their relation to social change. They provide a powerful analysis of social categories as linguistic and dynamic constructions that both enable and limit social action. Their approach nevertheless has some problems that can also be attributed to the SIT paradigm itself; in their theorization of social identification, certain determining factors of subjectivity, such as desire and enjoyment, are overlooked. This point leads us to the limitations of the discursive approach more generally in its theorization identity and intergroup relations.

Limitations to the discursive approach

The discursive perspective in social psychology offers an alternative framework that takes seriously language and the constructed nature of identities and intergroup relations. This perspective nevertheless provides a limited understanding for at least three reasons. Firstly, it is mute on the question of *why* categories can come to have such an effect on people's minds and actions. Why and how do discursively constructed categories come to 'move' people? How can, for example, some counter-hegemonic discourses manage to mobilize people? Secondly, much of the discursive work, despite being critical of the rationalistic assumptions of the SIT approach, "participates in a rationalist fallacy that itself 'flattens out' situations of great emotional complexity, of intense feeling" (Frosh, 2002, p. 189). Staying largely at the level of knowledge and discourse, these studies refuse to take seriously the *affective* nature of group identities, intergroup relations and resistance. There is no illustration of the 'sticky elements' of discourse that permeate seemingly rational accounts. Discursive representations are emphasized over and above the dynamic processes of identity that give them force and hold them in place. These dynamic processes cannot simply be explained as discourse. "There is an outside to the world of discourse" (Frosh, 1999, p. 386). Thirdly, although contradiction, negotiation and tension are highlighted, the discursive perspective does not *adequately* account for the less than explicit, less than conscious ambivalence, ambiguousness and the overdetermined nature of social phenomena. We mentioned earlier that SIT research has been criticized for neglecting the ironic aspect of social activity. The same can be said about some discursive research that, although it acknowledges ambivalence, inconsistency and contradiction, does not sufficiently elaborate on the nature of this ambivalence and its relation to subjectivity. Moreover, despite being careful not to fall back to a form of voluntarism, the work on counter-hegemonic talk, the emphasis on the 'critical' reasoning and the 'agency' of the subject tends to end up reinforcing voluntarism. Identities can be reconstructed by means of discursive, rhetorical and argumentative strategies, and largely through conscious and voluntaristic efforts. The point of analysis is often an active subject who is able to detach themselves from the discursive and power struggles in which they find themselves, to easily separate themselves from representations that otherize and exclude. An alternative theory to the SIT tradition should be more suspicious of constructions of authenticity, agency and self (see Parker, 1989). A particular absence in much of the discursive research concerns the study of how *resistance itself may generate certain counter-productive fixities of identity* (see Chapters 6 and 7 in this book). In order to address these problems researchers need to take seriously the unconscious, affective and even the non-discursive component of group identities.

Some researchers have attempted to do just that, and worked to complement the discursive perspective by applying psychoanalytic concepts in order to understand how and why individual subjects *invest* in or oppose certain identities or discursive positions (e.g. Frosh, Phoenix & Pattman, 2003; Gough, 2004; Hollway & Jefferson, 2000). These studies are presented as a critique against a discourse analytic approach in psychology that implies an "impoverished notion of subjectivity" where the social dimension and language are favoured "whilst the individual is suppressed" (Gough, 2004, p. 247). Frosh et al. (2003), for example, argue for an analysis that illustrates the "powerful effects of social discourses and the agentic struggle of particular subjects" (p. 42). Their aim is to focus on the specificity of subjectivity, to unearth "the subject as agent" (p. 42). These studies therefore have a 'local' analytic focus in that they apply Kleinian or object relations psychoanalytic theories to investigate why particular *individuals* take on or negotiate specific subject positions available in culture and discourse. In this sense, the emphasis is not only on how contested identities are used and renegotiated in discourse and language, but also on what relationship this process has to the affective and unconscious world of individuals.

It is, however, a very dubious practice to extend psychoanalytic techniques beyond the clinic for use in research interviews to interpret individuals' talk (see Frosh, 2008; Hook, 2008b; Parker, 2005). Psychoanalytic practice typically requires that someone is in analysis for a considerable period of time, and the analyst needs to be fully trained. Although the 'Kleinian' discursive research has been important in pinpointing how certain aspects of discourse are heavily affectively loaded, intertwined with intense investment, using psychoanalytic tools to interpret interview participants' 'inner world' and biography can be problematic. According to Frosh (2008), applying the clinical method in research interviews not only "does a disservice to psychoanalysis but also raises epistemological and practical problems" (p. 419). Further, this approach can be argued to individualize, essentialize, pathologize and disempower interview participants, and it can be challenged for falling prey to psychological reductionism (Parker, 2005) as well as for being ethically questionable. The previously discussed discursive research studies on identity and categorization do not elaborate on the issue of subjectivity, they depict subjects as uncomplicated and 'blank', but the above-mentioned 'psychoanalytic discourse' studies that attempt to circumvent the 'blank subjectivity' problem risk adopting a humanist understanding of subjects as independent voluntary agents. Even though the aim of this type of research is to avoid the familiar social–individual division, their use of 'agency' as more or less unproblematic and the focus on how discourses are used at the 'individual' level, might in fact reproduce social–individual dualism (see Parker, 2005 for a critique of this paradigm).

The discursive approach in social psychology discussed earlier dismisses many aspects of the SIT (Reicher and Hopkins' 1996, 2001a, and 2001b body of research is an exception) and appears to simply translate some limited number of SIT's 'cognitive' notions, such as categorization, in terms of processes in language. Although it has been fundamental in highlighting language and the broader socio-symbolic infrastructure of groups and intergroup behaviour, the discursive perspective has failed to unpack and develop in detail many concepts of the SIT approach, and especially the social change aspect. This book embraces a discursive understanding of identity and intergroup relations, but combines this with Lacanian theory, in ways not dissimilar to some work outside the discipline of social psychology (e.g. Bracher, 1993), in order to examine in detail some of the main postulates of the SIT paradigm.

Given that concepts such as desire are used to demonstrate what is lacking and problematic in the SIT paradigm, this approach can of course be accused of falling back into a universalistic understanding of group identities and intergroup relations. Indeed, a Lacanian perspective would care less about the content and meaning of discourse than the way discourse structures subjectivity and desire. It should, however, be argued here that although aspects of subjectivity, such as desire, are understood as universal

characteristics of the human being, each case of intra- or intergroup behaviour should be viewed as historically and socially embedded.
Psychoanalytic concepts "must be viewed as neither timeless nor arbitrary,
rather as historically specific, contingent upon a backdrop of particular
discursive practices" (Hook, 2006, p. 215). Unlike the SIT paradigm, the
approach in this book is not to predict the nature of group identities or
intergroup relations. We as social theorists can only hypothesize the kind
of psychological dynamics that may be involved in group identification, or in
specific cases of intergroup relations. We can speculate, never predict, and
even when speculating, we would be wary of the ways our theories may
work to produce specific forms of 'subjectivities' or 'truths'. Of course,
Lacanian theory *does* include certain assumptions about human nature, but it
"lends itself more readily to an understanding of subjectivity as socially
produced and regulated, while retaining a notion of subjective agency, albeit
not rational or consciously controlled" (Georgaca, 2005, p. 77). Let us note
that not everything can be explained by discourse (or cultural norms and
so on). Therefore, "discourse analysts should take Lacan seriously" (Pavón
Cuéllar, 2010, p. xv). In order to better grasp group identity and intergroup
relations we need a more elaborate understanding of the nature of subjectivity.
This would include a consideration of how categories and intergroup relations, often constructed in hegemonic discourses and sites of power, become
bound up with elements of subjectivity. We should thus "investigate how
power and desire (or fear, anxiety, fantasy) are simultaneously produced ...
and produced at least partly within the machinery of subjectivity that is not
entirely accessible to rational discursive consciousness" (Hook, 2006,
p. 215).

Categories as signifiers of the symbolic

We have said that the discursive critique of the SIT approach is limited and it
reworks only certain aspects of the theory. In this last section of the chapter, a
couple of Lacanian concepts that overlap with the discursive perspective are
introduced. The following chapters introduce more of Lacan's theory while
deconstructing and reworking some of the main concepts of the SIT
tradition.

Lacan certainly does not do away with the issue of discourse and language. On the contrary, "discursive theory seems to be already included in
Lacanian theory" (Branney, 2008, p. 585). Lacan states that it is "the world of
words that creates the worlds of things" (Lacan, 1977, p. 72). Language is
seen as fundamental in the construction of humans and their relation to things
in the world, including other humans. Language and discourse exist, in
Lacanian theory, in a specific field within human reality. They are positioned

in the field of the *symbolic*. The symbolic is the socio-discursive domain: it is equal to language. It is therefore the institutional network of a given culture, the very objectivity of society (the symbolic is discussed further in the next chapter). As we have said, the discursive perspective considers mental processes or phenomena as operating in and through language. Indeed, the SIT paradigm's cognitive notion of categorization (a mechanism that supposedly accentuates similarities among stimuli belonging to the same category and differences among stimuli belonging to different categories) should be understood as operating within the symbolic. Cognitive mechanisms are conditioned by the symbolic. They are symbolic mechanisms. In fact, "human cognition does not exist without the symbolic order of language" (Pavón Cuéllar, 2010, p. 69). Therefore, the 'cognitive' process of categorization should be understood in terms of the symbolic process of *signifiers*.

Lacan (1977) takes the notion of the signifier as an element of a sign from the linguist Ferdinand de Saussure (1974). He nevertheless departs from Saussure when he prioritizes the signifier over the signified. A signifier is the basic element of language or the symbolic. Language should be understood in a broad sense. A signifier could therefore be not only a word but also a phrase, a smell, a touch, a sound or a person. Many discourse theorists would possibly agree that *it is signifiers that are involved in categorization processes*. Indeed,

> since categories are nothing more than signifiers implying structural relations between signifiers, categorization is just a form of signifierization that reduces things and people to *signifying categories* such as 'black', 'red', 'revolutionary', etc.
>
> (Pavón Cuéllar, 2010, p. 69)

A signifier alone is meaningless. It only gains meaning in relation to other signifiers. It *temporarily* signifies through its differential relation to other signifiers. The meaning of the category 'man' is thus only comprehensible in relation to the category 'woman'. Therefore, we could easily translate "a network of intergroup categorizations" (Tajfel et al., 1971, p. 153) or "a system of categorical social relations" (Reicher & Hopkins, 2001b, p. 48) into a *system of signifiers*. Signifiers structure our world; they construct subjects' relation to their groups and other groups. We can indeed state that categorizations as signifiers "give order and coherence to the social situation" (Tajfel et al., 1971, p. 153). It is with signifiers that we attempt to represent, 'fix' and create a unitary and coherent identity. Signifiers are therefore "the materials of identity" (Vanheule & Verhaeghe, 2009, p. 405).

Understanding categories in terms of signifiers, as elements of the symbolic, implies – contrary to some discursive perspectives – that we *do* need to take categories for granted in some ways. In Lacanian theory, the symbolic is historic and objective, it is the very infrastructure of society, and thus exists *before* and *after* any individual or any single group. In a sense, categories or groups are *already constructed* by the symbolic; they are already materialized. Opposing some of the discursive positions, a Lacanian framework shows us that people can be 'victims' of categorization processes because they are to an extent the targets, the products; the victims of the symbolic. The symbolic, as the discursive and institutional infrastructure of a given society, conditions intergroup relations. Chapter 5 elaborates this argument using the minimal group experiments as illustration. It shows how the results of the experiments can be understood as effects of the symbolic. It demonstrates how the behaviour of the participants in the experiment can be viewed as products of the discourse of the experimenter.

Categories, or the symbolic, are nevertheless also *continually reproduced* and sometimes challenged and negotiated. We can therefore state that categories are already given, but will need to be reproduced through the identification acts of subjects. These acts should not be understood in cognitive or voluntaristic terms. Lacanian theory depicts the subject as extremely complicated; the subject does not consist of an essence, nor does it have any unproblematic internally located 'motivations'. These themes will be expanded further in the following chapters.

Conclusion

This chapter has reviewed some of the main challenges to the SIT perspective. To summarize: The SIT approach to identity, group belonging and intergroup relations has been criticized for giving too much power to individual, cognitive and rational processes that are believed to be universal, and for not taking wider historical and cultural dynamics seriously. The neglect of the role of language and discourse in constructing categories and determining our relations to groups has been a major focus of critique. The discursive perspective highlights the importance of language, but many researchers within this perspective disregard much of the ideas of the SIT tradition, and without offering satisfactory alternative concepts. SCT and SIT include very detailed illustrations of the relation between the individual and the group, and the various ways and circumstances in which groups relate to each other. Rather than simply rejecting the SIT paradigm, the rest of the book unpacks and reworks its main concepts with the help of Lacanian theory. Along the way, it will also elaborate on some of the issues and critiques raised in this chapter.

3 The category, not the self

SCT "is concerned with the antecedents, nature and consequences of psychological group formation: how does some collection of individuals come to define and feel themselves to be a social group and how does shared group membership influence their behavior?" (Turner, 1985, p. 78). The theory explains intragroup behaviour in terms of self-categorization. Intragroup behaviour is defined as "interaction between two or more individuals that is governed by a common or shared social self-categorisation or social identity" (Hogg & Abrams, 1988, p. 93). This chapter argues that SCT's cognitive illustration of group behaviour fails to address the subjective nature of the relation between the individual and the group. Not only does it downplay historical, cultural and discursive factors (as discussed in the previous chapter), but also, its depiction of the individual–group relationship as one that is analogous to mechanics is unsatisfactory. In order to rework some of the main arguments of SCT, this chapter makes recourse to theorists who utilize Lacanian concepts in their theorization of people's relation to modern society and ideology. The predominant concepts used here will be the symbolic Other, ego-ideal, ideal-ego, desire and alienation. Generally speaking, SCT's idea of the 'individual-category relation' should be understood in terms of the subject's affiliation to the socio-symbolic field. It should be perceived as the very mechanism that produces individual human beings capable of communicating and interacting within a social environment.

From the early days of Freud, psychoanalysis has been concerned with the relation between the subject and the collective, between the individual and the social. Rather than promoting a cognitive or predominantly discursive understanding of the individual–social relation, psychoanalysis views the latter as a deeply affective, yet complicated, symbolic bond. Similar to SCT, however, the Lacanian perspective emphasizes that "the experience of identity is a result of the mechanism of 'identification'" (Vanheule & Verhaeghe, 2009, p. 392) – although in Lacan subjective experience is prioritized over cognitive computations. Moreover, rather than being preformed, the subject is *produced* through identification with an 'external' entity. This entity, which we can say is a social category, is of course itself subject to historical variability and contestation, but it is through this identification process that the subject comes into being. It is therefore not the 'self' that is the predominant factor in group processes. The *category*, understood in terms of the signifier, should be viewed as primary. The present chapter unpacks the following SCT concepts: the psychological group, referent informational influence, group prototype, the self-concept and depersonalization. Each of these is reworked and their relation to Lacanian ideas of subjectivity is discussed.

Psychological group and the symbolic

SCT is concerned with a problem that is as old as social psychology itself, that is, the connection between the subject and society, or more specifically, the individual's relationship to the group. The SIT tradition was certainly not the first to discover the notion that a person's mind and behaviour fluctuate between a 'personal' and a 'collective' frame of reference. This is a longstanding problem in philosophy: to understand the relations between the 'personal' and the 'collective'. SCT researchers do nevertheless ask the question that had, covertly or overtly, concerned the very early group theorists such as Freud (1959) and Le Bon (1896): "does the group possess a mental unity or reality *sui generis*?" (Turner et al., 1987, p. 3). In other words, does the group have its own mind? Is the group an organism which functions beyond, or independently of, its members? Or is it simply a collection of individuals that compose it? Unlike much classical social psychology, SCT does not explain the group as an aggregate of individual members. Neither does it totally agree with Freud and Le Bon's 'group mind' thesis. SCT does, however, illuminate the distinctive role of the *social psychological group*; it highlights the role of *social categories* in shaping people's thinking and behaviour.

SCT developed the idea – which stems from some earlier work on groups in social psychology – that "interdependent individuals form a social-psychological system which transforms qualitatively their character as individuals and gives rise to '*supra-individual*' properties" (Turner, 1987, p. viii, emphasis added). These properties could be said to constitute an entity in its own right and cannot be explained in terms of any individual quality. Neither is this entity exactly equal to the mean average of attitudes and values of the individuals in a group:

> The group process produces distinctive, emergent normative tendencies, inexplicable as derivatives of the individual properties of members…
> the relations between members seem in some puzzling way to be

mediated by their membership in the group, producing social norms with 'whole-properties' different from the sum of their parts.

(Turner et al., 1987, p. 87)

SCT is here covertly relying on something akin to the notion of the *symbolic*. The 'supra-individual', 'whole-properties', are symbolic properties, they are signifiers, and could therefore be translated into the Lacanian 'symbolic system'. This is exactly the system that contains the social norms of the group. Signifiers are, as we have already mentioned, an element of the symbolic. They are therefore elements of the *Other* – often also referred to as the *big Other*. "The big Other operates at a symbolic level" (Žižek, 2006, p. 9). As the Turner et al. quote above indirectly suggests, every group puts into operation something which is similar to the *symbolic Other*. *It is the linguistic and symbolic 'properties' of the group that make up the Other*. Like language, the symbolic exists before any single person; it exists beyond individual group members (even though it does not exist independently of the members' continuous activity). This is partly why it is referred to as the Other; it exists 'outside' individual consciousness, and is Other to any single person in the group. The big Other as the "entirety of the symbolic domain" (Hook, 2008a, p. 55) pre-exists individuals. It is a 'treasury of signifiers' that can be understood in terms of a collection of norms, values and standards specific to a group. The group – national, religious, or political, for example – is of course composed of separate individuals, but as a *symbolic function* it is qualitatively different to the individuals that compose it. Although the symbolic pre-exists individuals, "the gestures of symbolization are entwined with and embedded in the process of collective practice" (Žižek, 2006, p. 15). In other words, the practices and actions of the group ensure the existence of the Other. Within a religious group, for example, certain rituals (going to the church, praying) guarantee, for the group, the existence of the Other as personified in the figure of 'God'. This implies that rather than existing within the realm of cognition, the symbolic is manifested in collective discursive practice.

The symbolic, then, can be understood as "society's unwritten constitution" (Žižek, 2006, p. 8). It is *the network of social and institutional structures and practices underlying a given group*. The symbolic Other is the social substance itself; it is a "supra-agency" (Hook, 2008a, p. 55). It is the very principle of a trans-subjective social network that co-ordinates a collective. Every group believes in such 'supra-individual' Other as a means of legitimating certain values. Every group "has the effect – at least if we are to successfully participate, communicate within its means – of installing such a point of authority and appeal" (Hook, 2008a, p. 60). This Other, we could also say, is the unconscious of the group. The elements of the unconscious are collective and shared by members of a group "because of similar formative

experiences attributable to inhabiting the same culture and discourses"
(Bracher, 1993, p. 48). The unconscious is trans-individual because it
constitutes the common pool of cultural signifiers and discourses.

The hypothetical nature of the Lacanian Other is difficult to accommodate
within an SCT mode of reasoning. Within a cognitive and empirical framework, it would be hard to accept the idea that the Other "exists only in so far
as subjects *act as if it exists*" (Žižek, 2006, p. 10). Although the Other is the
trans-subjective network of group values, it is also the outcome of assumption. This is the paradox of the Other: "The Other is at the same time lacking,
a domain of presumption and fiction, and yet, it nonetheless remains the
anchoring point that a given society relies upon to maintain its coherence"
(Hook, 2008a, p. 63). On the one hand, what is commonly called 'group
coherence' in SCT is an impossibility. Individuals can never fully identify
with the group or with each other, and they can never perfectly communicate
with each other without some distortion or interruption of meaning. A
number of individuals may, for example, come together within the social
category 'British', but each individual may have different ideas of what
'Britishness' may be. Full identification with a social category and a perfectly joint co-ordination between individuals in a group is impossible. On
the other hand, this impossibility is what gives rise to the Other, as the point
of certainty, authority and coherence. It is also this impossibility that turns a
series of separate, aggregate individuals into a 'supra-individual' collectivity.
"The very impossibility of ... a knowing of others, of ... a perfected
communicative interchange, of the social mass being jointly coordinated,
gives rise to a virtual supplement – a kind of spiritual substance – which goes
some way to helping us negotiate this impossibility" (Hook, 2008a, p. 64).

In SCT, explicit categorization of individuals as group members is the only
necessary condition for group behaviour. The "primacy of social categorization" (Hogg & McGarty, p. 20) is emphasized, and the focus is directed away
from individual reasons (for example, personality, need satisfaction or the
attainment of individual goals) as determining factors for behaving in terms
of the group. SCT researchers sometimes understand social categorization as a
function of "preformed culturally available classification" (Turner et al., 1987,
p. 51), and they often claim "individual people are born into a particular society
and thus social categories are largely pre-existent *vis-à-vis* individuals" (Hogg
& Abrams, 1988, p. 15). These socially and historically structured categories
become internalized and cognitively stored. The "social group" is understood
"in cognitive terms, as an internalized cognitive representation of the group"
(Hogg & Abrams, 1988, p. 105). Thus, although the cultural and historical
nature of categories is acknowledged, cognitive powers predominate. From
our Lacanian framework, it would be the symbolic, or more precisely the
signifier, that would be the primary factor in group behaviour. As we claimed

in the previous chapter, the category itself is a signifier. This implies that we would understand categories as existing within the realm of language, beyond cognition and any individual person, although categories may play a part in structuring individual cognition. The 'cognitive representation of the group' should be understood in terms of the signifier. When SCT researchers talk about "allegiance to the group rather than the individuals in the group" (Hogg & Abrams, 1988, p. 92), we can understand this as 'allegiance to the signifier'; the group as understood as a signifier. It is, thus, the symbolic that mediates group behaviour. 'Acting in terms of the cognitive representation of the group', or 'acting in terms of the category', could be understood, from our Lacanian framework, as 'acting in terms of the signifier'. This is the same as saying that somebody acts in the *name* of the group rather than for the sake of the individuals within a group – individuals who they never even meet in the case of large-scale groups such as a national group. What is responsible for the psychological formation of the group is therefore the *signifier*. An American soldier who is fighting in Iraq is doing so for the signifier 'The United States' (and less so for the hundreds of millions of individuals happening to live in the geographical area labelled 'The United States'), and would even accept to die for the sake of this signifier. Of course, a soldier may feel affinity with the actual individuals living in the United States, but he or she will always do so via a signifier such as 'The United States'. If categories were understood as signifiers, we would – following SCT – ascribe explanatory power to categories. Indeed, certain exceptional categories often have a powerful influence on people.

Referent informational influence and the big Other

We have shown how the 'psychological group' can be understood in terms of the symbolic and the signifier. SCT's notion of *referent informational influence* can be understood along similar lines. SCT revises some of the earlier social influence studies in social psychology by showing how social influence is a function of shared group membership that offers members a shared frame of reference to interpret the world. Membership in a reference group determines what are 'correct' and 'incorrect' ways of thinking and behaving (Turner, 1991). A reference group (or a psychological group)

> is defined as one that is psychologically significant for the members, to which they relate themselves subjectively … i.e. with which they compare to evaluate themselves, their abilities, performances, opinions, etc., and from which they take their rules, standards and beliefs about appropriate conduct and attitudes.

> (Turner et al., 1987, p. 2)

Researchers within the SCT framework argue that group phenomena such as altruism, cohesion, and, in particular, social influence, depend on a reference group. Referent informational influence is responsible for conformity to group norms, and it "operates through self-categorization (identification)" (Hogg & Abrams, 1988, p. 175). People first define themselves as belonging to a salient social category and then assign to themselves the norms and values of that category. That is, psychological group formation is a necessary condition for social influence: "the psychological group seems to be at the beginning and not the end of the influence process; its precondition, not its product" (Turner et al., 1987, p. 40). The mere knowledge that one belongs to a specific category is enough for influence to take place. Categorization is thus a key factor in power and influence. When we categorize ourselves into a group we conform to the ideology of the group, which consists of norms that provide crucial information about appropriate ways to think and behave. Therefore, the behaviour or attitude of another person

> is persuasive to the degree that it represents and participates in some shared, consensual reaction stereotypically associated with an in-group self-category and hence is perceived as valid, correct, competent … which in turn leads to *its perception as appropriate, desirable, expected, something one ought to believe or do.*
>
> (Turner et al., 1987, p. 76, emphasis added)

Intragroup norms have an effect on the group member because they represent what is acceptable and desirable in the relevant category, they signify who one should be and how one should think and behave in order to be accepted, *recognized* as a group member. Categorization – or, from our perspective, the symbolic function – is here given priority. What seems to have a significant effect on the individual is not simply another group member, but the norms and values, a more abstract notion of the rules and laws of the relevant social group: "the behavior of others provides information about appropriate attitudes and actions in so far as it exemplifies the norms of some reference group" (Turner et al., 1987, p. 72). The reference group becomes, we could say, the symbolic Other that "acts like a yardstick against which I can measure myself" (Žižek, 2006, p. 9). Social consensus within a reference group comes to be taken as objective facts: "the 'facts' of individual perception and judgment – that the earth is a globe, that an elephant is larger than a mouse … are themselves social norms, based on the prior or current, explicit or implicit agreements of appropriate reference groups" (Turner et al., 1987, p. 74). According to SCT, the group member perceives social consensus about a given issue as that which is "*objectively* required, correct, valid, demanded, appropriate" (Turner et al., 1987, p. 72). Only with the help of others, and specifically qualified others – that is, members of a reference group – can the individual verify whether what he or she perceives is correct. In other words, the reference group, the Other, validates the perception and the experiences of the individual. Let us, however, remind ourselves that from our Lacanian framework, we cannot accept that group belonging and conformity to groups are simply "inextricable products of a cognitive process of categorization" (Hogg & Abrams, 1988, p. 173).

What the SCT overlooks is firstly that conformity is a linguistic and symbolic process. One is 'influenced' by the discourse of the reference group: one can only make sense of the 'objective' events or 'things' in the world via communication; using or making recourse to language. In fact, since it is the signifiers of the group that 'think' for us, language of the group is what produces 'correct perception' (see Parker, 2003; Pavón Cuéllar, 2010). Secondly, for the individual member, the reference group becomes the source of authority, and people often accept anything so long as it comes from a source that is invested with authority. "The content of a message is not as important as the source from which it emanates" (Stavrakakis, 2008, p. 1046). The presupposition that somebody is in command is in fact characteristic of all social experience; human beings tend to want and search for authority because "without someone in command reality disintegrates" (Stavrakakis, 2008, p. 1048). In this sense, the reference group as the Other is the 'subject-supposed-to-know'. The subject-supposed-to know "functions as embodiment of authority and knowledge" (Hook, 2008a, p. 5). This involves "a sense of the *acceptance of what others accept* – and have done so as a means of avoiding the uncertainty of the (our) social being" (Hook, 2008a, p. 65). The subject searches for validation and solidity in the reference group. As a way to escape uncertainty, we tend to think that the symbolic 'knows' the truth about us; we believe the group is supposed to know what we should think and do. Therefore, accepting what others accept, rather than being driven by cognitive processes, is primarily *determined by the need to escape anxiety and uncertainty*. Something similar to this idea can perhaps be found in the 'uncertainty reduction hypothesis' (e.g. Hogg, 2000; Hogg & Abrams, 1993). This is a more recent development in SCT that acknowledges the reduction of uncertainty as a powerful motive for human action. Psychoanalysis would add that uncertainty characterizes, at a deeper level, the whole being of the subject. Uncertainty is related to the lack of knowledge of one's place in the world, or more precisely, it is about not knowing what one is for the Other. It is the attempt to avoid this traumatic and unbearable experience of 'not knowing', or not 'being anybody', that is one major determinant of identification and conformity (the next chapter discusses how this process is related to desire and recognition).

The following are a summary of the two aspects of the symbolic big Other that we need to bear in mind before we move on:

1   The Other is a *point* of reflexivity, the structurally necessary point of reference from which one sees and judges oneself. It is the perspective of the reference group.
2   The Other is the locus, the place, that routinely comes to be filled up with signifiers (the values and ideals) of a group. It comes to be occupied by a set of *contents*, and functions as a store-house of ideals.

Prototypes and ego-ideals

In SCT the values of the group are known as prototypes. People represent their groups in terms of prototypes. The prototype "is a subjective sense of the defining attributes of a social category" (Hornsey, 2008, p. 209). Prototypes "guide perception, self-conception, and action" (Hogg, 2001, p. 187). An individual member's prototypicality is the extent to which he or she is perceived as representative of stereotypical attributes of the group. The more a group member's behaviour or attitudes are normative or exemplify some valued characteristic of the group, the more this member will be liked by the group: "a person is evaluated positively to the degree that he or she approximates the ideal member of a positive group" (Turner et al., 1987, p. 58). In other words, the group prototype is the group ideal.

From our Lacanian framework, we would understand group prototypes as defined within language by the use of signifiers. These signifiers are *ego-ideals* that delineate the 'ideal member'. *These ego-ideals are found in the language or discourse of the group.* "Ego-ideals are symbolic elements that a subject takes from the discourse of the [O]ther ... they are nothing but privileged discursive elements" (Vanheule & Verhaeghe, 2009, p. 397). An ego-ideal could thus be understood as "the prototype that is being used as the standard" (Turner et al., 1987, p. 58) that group members are called upon to live up to. In other words, ego-ideals are the shared norms, values and expectations of the reference group as the Other. Hence, we could say that with the Other we mean the *point* from which we judge ourselves (the perspective of the group), while ego-ideals or prototypes are the symbolic *content* of values and norms that fills out, animates this virtual supposition of the Other. While the Other is a *position*, a presumed point (or perspective) of appeal to authority, knowledge, validation, embodied in the symbolic, the ego-ideal, by contrast, functions to give the subject a sense of unity, as a benchmark for his or her achievements (or lack thereof). The culture or ideology of a group works largely by the expectations or ego-ideals of the Other.

The identification that the member makes with these ego-ideals, the prototypes of the group, is *symbolic identification* with the discourse of the Other. Once given a place in a group, members view themselves as part of the same collectivity, with shared attitudes and worldviews because they all view themselves from, or identify with, some or other variation of the Other typifying that social location. It is the perspective of the ego-ideal, subject to a degree of subjective latitude, which is inscribed in the members: *the group has an influence on thinking and behaviour because the ego-ideal signifiers of the group (of the Other) have been engraved in the structure of the subject.* We can now see how ego-ideals, just like SCT's prototypes, work to frame action; they both enable and limit action.

Turner et al. note that

> the most prototypical (normative, valued) position is not the sum or mean of ingroup responses, nor an individual property of the member holding it, but is a higher order, category property, reflecting the views of all members. The prototypical member's persuasiveness, perceived competence, leadership, the perceived validity of their information, etc., are mediated by and based on his or her membership in the group as a 'whole'.
>
> (Turner et al., 1987, p. 88)

As the above quote covertly implies, we need to make a distinction between the prototypical position or 'the category property' (which is the position of the Other) and the 'prototypical member' (the Other's ideal personified in a group member). The leader or the most influential member in a group is usually the member that best personifies the ego-ideal of the Other, or, in the language of SCT, the one that best embodies the prototypical position. SCT theorizes the prototypical position as that position which represents the group as a whole. "The most prototypical member is the person who is simultaneously most different to the out-group and least different to the in-group" (Hogg & McGarty, 1990, p. 16). However, we must emphasize that the prototypical position, although representing the group, is *different* to other positions in the group. Hogg (2001) alludes to this difference when he states, "there is a clearly perceived gradient of prototypicality within the group, with some people perceived to be more prototypical than others" (p. 189). The *distinct* position of the leader is evidenced by the paradoxical fact that leaders can "diverge most radically from the views, behaviors and so on, of the group as a whole" and they can often "enjoy a degree of individual freedom and idiosyncrasy not enjoyed by their followers" (Hogg & Abrams, 1988, p. 114). In fact, from a Lacanian perspective, the *actual* leader of a group, the one that has most influence on the mind and behaviour of the group, is the position that is radically Other to anybody else in the group. While the leader occupies the position of the Other (the big Other), fellow group members are merely mirror images of each other.

The self-concept and ideal-egos

SCT confuses categorization by the Other as a *symbolic* identification with *ego-ideals*, and *self*-categorization as an *imaginary* identification with *ideal-egos*. Ego-ideals are different to ideal-egos, even though the two overlap in many ways. Ideal-egos are body images which appear lovable to us, and for this reason they entail a narcissistic component. Imaginary ideal-ego identification is with the image that signifies *who we want to be*. The "self-concept" as "the set of cognitive representations of self available to a person" (Turner et al., 1987, p. 44) is imaginary. This is because the self-concept (another term for it would be the ego) is, in the words of Turner et al., composed of "specific self-*images*" (p. 44, emphasis added). These self-images are the images in which we like to see ourselves; they are our ideal-egos.

Turner et al. (1987) state "attraction to others is a direct function of their perceived similarity to one's ideal self" (p. 58). Attraction to others involves then a process of evaluating the 'self': "the self is evaluated at some level … by the same process that leads to liking or disliking for others" (Turner et al., 1987, p. 57). SCT also presents the very psychoanalytic idea that when we evaluate others, we are at the same time judging whether they are "'self' or not 'self' " (Turner et al., 1987, p. 59). Whether one likes somebody depends on whether one perceives them to be similar, in, for example, attitudes, goals and values, to oneself, "and in particular to one's ideal self" (Turner et al., 1987, p. 59). Group cohesion is therefore a function of *perceived* similarity between self and others. From our Lacanian framework, 'the self', which is an imaginary construction built out of ideal-egos, determines our evaluation of other people. Attraction to others is an assessment of the degree to which others match our ideal-ego. Indeed, ideal-egos bring people together and form an imaginary sense of unity: "This is how individuals congregate simultaneously *around* an 'ideal-ego' " (Pavón Cuéllar, 2010, p. 15).

SCT researchers argue that "cognitive representations of the self take the form, amongst others, of *self-categorizations*, i.e. cognitive groupings of oneself and some class of stimuli as the same (identical, similar, equivalent, interchangeable, and so on) in contrast to some other class of stimuli" (Turner et al., 1987, p. 44). But perceived similarity to group members is nothing but an *imaginary* similarity to fellow members. It involves *recognizing oneself in the image of ingroup members*. In this process, there is no distinction between the self and ingroup members: "self and other become stereotypically interchangeable" (Hogg & Abrams, 1988, p. 107). Identification with fellow group members merges self and other, and one can be substituted for the other. The 'other' here is therefore not really an other. This process exaggerates the imaginary similarities within our group and differences between our group and other groups. *Self-categorization is then an imaginary process.* It involves identifying with an image which appears both lovable to us, and like us. This image can, however, also become the basis for rivalry and aggression (Lacan, 1977). The imaginary bond between individuals within a group is vulnerable. A fellow group member can easily turn into a target for aggression, jealousy, distrust and hatred.

As we have argued, the imaginary other is not really an other. The 'real' Other is the language of the group. This is what is meant by symbolic identification; it is identification with something which is Other. Symbolic identification is with *the position from which we are being seen*, and from which we appear lovable. This is identification with the position of the reference group, the point from which our ideal-ego is approved. In this sense, 'self-images' are also symbolic: "symbolic elements determine the adoption of self-images" (Vanheule & Verhaege, 2009, p. 397). The subject's identification with these images makes him or her lovable in the gaze of the Other (as the reference group). It is thus from the point of the ego-ideal that the body image (the ideal-ego or the self-concept) makes sense.

The relationship between imaginary and symbolic identification can be demonstrated with Freud's (1959) theory of groups. Freud is concerned with subjects' identification with each other in the context of large groups or ideological affiliations. He claims that the people in a group identify with each other because of "an important emotional common quality; and we may suspect that this common quality lies in the nature of the tie with the leader" (p. 137). The identifications between the members of the group are different to the identification the members make with the leader:

> A ... group ... is a number of individuals who have put one and the same object in the place of their ego-ideal and have consequently identified themselves with one another in their ego.
>
> (Freud, 1959, p. 147)

Following Freud, we can suppose that identification with similar others is an identification with imaginary ideal-egos, and identification with prototypes is identification with the symbolic ego-ideals of the reference group. To clarify, the identification I make with fellow group members is *imaginary*, because it entails an identification with others who are like me – while identification with the leader or the prototype is *symbolic*, because this involves identification with someone who is not like me, and who occupies a different position to anybody else in the group. As Žižek states,

> we could say that in imaginary identification we imitate the other at the level of resemblance – we identify ourselves with the image of the other inasmuch as we are 'like him,' while in symbolic identification we identify ourselves with the other precisely at a point at which he is inimitable, at the point which eludes resemblance.
>
> (Žižek, 1989, p. 109)

Identification with prototypes (ego-ideals) is not a matter of how we see ourselves in images, but *how we are seen* by that Other which gives these images an order and which provides the co-ordinates according to which they become viewable, prioritized, important versus non-important.

The self in question

As we have stated, in SCT, categorization is an explanatory factor. However, despite attempting to highlight the distinguished role of the category in determining thinking and behaviour, the 'self' tends to gain a privileged status. The notion of 'self-categorization' puts the 'self' at the forefront. It implies that the self is at the beginning of the group process, that it exists independently of the group, and the norms and values of the latter have an impact on individuals only once they have categorized *themselves* into that group. Although the 'self' is not an altogether irrelevant concept, it is subordinate to the Other. In a theory of group processes, it should be made absolutely clear that the Other – the psychological group or the linguistic properties relevant to a reference group – comes first. It is not a matter of *self*-categorization, but of *categorization by the Other*: categorization by language. Given that the social category itself exists within the symbolic field, we could state that the discursive ego-ideals of the Other "*determine* the subject" (Hook, 2008a, p. 55). This actually indicates that rather than focusing on a 'psychology' of groups, we would instead study how categories that matter for people's 'self understandings' – such as national, religious, or political categories – *produce* subjects, or a particular form of subjectivity, and how identification in turn feeds into and sustains these categories.

Self-categorization, which is the individual's definition of him or herself, is different to the definition of the subject by the socio-symbolic field of the Other. Psychoanalysis takes the unconscious seriously. Once the unconscious is being considered, "individual motivations to adopt certain self-categorizations and avoid others" (Hogg & Abrams, 1988, p. 26) can no longer be interpreted as a result of conscious will. Even when people 'choose' to, for example, categorize themselves in a specific group, they do not necessarily act consciously. An apparently 'conscious' choice can still be under the influence of unconscious motives. These motives do not exist 'within' individuals but are external to individuals. Given that "the unconscious is the discourse of the Other" (e.g. Lacan, 1977, p. 214), the individual making a seemingly conscious choice is under the influence of the symbolic Other, that is, an already existing and external system of categorizations. The unconscious is always in a sense beyond individuality; it is something which is 'out there' in society, in language, in the social structure and institutions of any culture, as well as in the psychic field of the subject. Thus, *self*-categorizations are never simply an action of the self; the 'self', which is a *fiction*, is always under the influence of the symbolic Other.

What is more, our self-concept, our *knowledge* of ourselves, is totally separate from what we *do*. In other words, our self-categorizations can completely contradict our everyday practices. A woman may, for example, self-categorize as a 'feminist', yet be obsessed with her body. She may, for example, undergo painful surgery or spend ours in the gym, making sure to produce a body that lives up to the predominant image of femininity that is the object of men's desire. She may see herself as a 'feminist' and identify with other feminists, but her obsessive behaviours in relation to her body are the very practices that reproduce patriarchy and the subordination of women. In fact, as researchers within the SIT paradigm very well know, feminism exists only as a comparison to, or in relation to, that which is not feminism, which we could say is patriarchy. In our example, 'patriarchy' is the reference group, or the symbolic Other. Now it becomes clearer why the reference group can be understood as the Other. We could say that the woman is *alienated* in the language of patriarchy; she is *alienated* in the Other.

Depersonalization and alienation

From our Lacanian perspective, we could say that the process of 'depersonalization' involves an experience of alienation. According to SCT, when the individual identifies with a group, they become 'depersonalized': they tend to see themselves as similar to other ingroup members. This involves a "*change* from the personal to the social level of identity" rather than a "'loss' of sense of individuality" (Turner et al., 1987, p. 51).

In Lacan, identification with the Other entails a gain in the signifier. This implies that the Other offers the subject an identity, a sense of unity and consistency. The SCT researchers Hogg and McGarty (1990) state that "the individual is perceptually and behaviorally depersonalized in terms of the relevant in-group prototype" (p. 13). We could say the symbolic Other imposes a set of ego-ideals (i.e. prototypes) in which the subject can recognize itself, and be recognized by others. However, in Lacan's much more radical theory, this "involves choosing one's own disappearance" (Fink, 2003, p. 246). From this perspective, therefore, the process does involve some loss, as well as a sense of alienation. The "experience of subjective identity is fundamentally alienated, inevitably constituted by alien elements derived from the [O]ther" (Vanheule & Verhaeghe, 2009, p. 399). Alienation is then a result of the subject identifying with elements that are external to him or herself, elements that originally belong to some Other. In other words, depersonalization should be understood in its proper Lacanian way as the disappearance of the subject behind the signifier (i.e. category or prototype).

This is why we cannot fully agree with the following statement by SCT theorists: "by asserting that self-categorizations function at different levels of abstraction makes both group and individual behavior 'acting in terms of self' " (Turner et al., 1987, p. ix). From our Lacanian framework, we would rather understand *both group and individual behaviour as acting in terms of the Other*. As we have emphasized, the 'self' is a fiction, a result of identification with, and alienation in, the Other. Confusingly, however, with the notion of depersonalization, SCT does acknowledge this predominance of the Other: depersonalization "represents a mechanism whereby individuals may act in terms of the social similarities and differences produced by the historical development of human society and culture" (Turner et al., 1987, p. 51). In other words, it involves a process whereby individuals 'act' in terms defined by the signifiers of the socio-symbolic Other.

Contrary to SCT's depiction of depersonalization as something positive rather than negative, we could state that depersonalization is *both* disabling and enabling. We can suppose that depersonalization is on the one hand disabling because it can stifle 'individual' liberation, and produce a sense of alienation. We need to take this very Freudian idea seriously even though the whole predicament of the SIT paradigm has been to move away from it. Identification with the signifiers of the group entails some suppression of 'individual' freedom. On the other hand, depersonalization or identification is enabling because it is, as SCT emphasizes, the foundation for co-operation, altruism and group cohesion. In fact, this is how subjects are produced: via identification with and alienation in the signifiers of the Other. As we discussed earlier, identification offers a sense of coherence and direction in the face of an otherwise fragmented and uncertain reality. Alienation in the signifiers of the reference group entails being given a place in the symbolic domain of the group. By identifying with ego-ideals there is a gain in the feeling of consistency; a sense of identity. Important to note though is the failure of signifiers of the group to ever fully represent the subject. There will always be a disjunction between the signifier (that is meant to represent the subject) and the vicissitudes, quandaries, deadlocks, anxieties and turmoil of the subject.

Before we move on, an important note about the term 'personal' needs to be made. In Lacanian theory, this term would not be used to refer to a "social encounter in which all the interaction that takes place is determined by the personal relationship between ... individuals and their individual characteristics" (Turner, 1999, p. 9), because such an encounter, which is not hooked to the symbolic, does not exist. Rather, 'personal' would be understood as that aspect most unique and exclusive to a subject. Lacan teaches us that even though the symbolic creates a shared 'life-world', and is thus irreducible to each 'individual' in a group, it is also true that no two individuals are the same; no two individuals have the same relation to the symbolic. Each individual's relation to this 'shared system' is unique. Even though many people can converge around the same signifier (e.g. 'Islam', 'Britain', 'the Market'), no two individuals have exactly the same kind of affiliation to this category (for example, there are many competing interpretations of 'Islam' by those who identify with it, and each subject's relation to 'Islam' is idiosyncratic). We can therefore suggest that contrary to some discursive perspectives discussed in the previous chapter, a 'personal' field of experience does indeed exist. This implies that 'depersonalization' is not a very appropriate term, because every individual's relation to the symbolic is in some sense very 'personal'.

Conclusion

Some of the predominant SCT notions of intragroup processes have been examined and reworked in this chapter. One of the main points was that categories as understood in terms of signifiers should be viewed as primary. What produces a 'psychological group' is the signifier. The symbolic defines people as part of a 'category', which means that, for example, 'British', 'Black', 'Muslim', are all signifiers assigned by language. Therefore, the symbolic, not the 'self', is the primary, 'explanatory' factor. What we can call 'agency' is on the side of the symbolic, not on the side of 'individuals', or the 'self'. Subjects are produced in relation to a reference group, as the symbolic Other, which imposes a series of ego-ideals (prototypes) which subjects identify with, and try to live up to. This chapter also suggested that depersonalization should be understood in terms of alienation. Identification with the group ideals is an alienated experience: the ideal of the symbolic Other gains priority; the 'self' becomes an Other. Giving priority and agency to the symbolic does not mean that people are nothing but passive victims of their groups, and that change is impossible. Firstly, by actively (not necessarily consciously or intentionally) identifying with signifiers of the Other, subjects have a significant role to play, and a responsibility, in reproducing categories. Secondly, rather than dismissing or ignoring change, a Lacanian perspective offers an alternative understanding of transformation. These issues will be discussed further in later chapters.

The discursive reinterpretation of the SIT framework completely disregards some of the fundamental components of subjectivity discussed in this chapter. For example, the discursive approach demonstrates how subjects and categories are constructed in discourse, but it does not include a theory of how discourse can create alienation. Furthermore, it does not consider why people conform to group norms, or how discourse can attach itself to subjects. We have seen in this chapter that the discourse of the group contains ego-ideals that subjects identify with. But why do people view themselves from the perspective of the ego-ideal of the reference group? This issue is discussed in the next chapter.

4   Whatever happened to "'hot' aspects of the group"?

This chapter continues to make recourse to Lacanian theorists who examine people's relation to society and community. The focus here will be on the affective components of group identification. The chapter pays attention to three questions that SCT has not answered in any satisfactory way: *Why do people conform to groups? How does a group of people bond with each other? Why do some categories and not others become salient?* The SIT perspective would approach these questions by depicting people either as passive victims of cognitive or perceptual computations, or active self-aware individuals with 'internal' motives. Rather than understanding group belonging in mechanistic terms (for example, in terms of 'cognition', 'perception, 'stimuli' or 'variables'), this chapter demonstrates how attachment to the group concerns recognition, love, desire, and enjoyment.

Tajfel and his followers, when they do discuss motivation or affect, tend to offer an individualistic and mechanistic understanding. Despite that these researchers address very 'irrational' phenomena such as prejudice and attachments to group ideals – attachments that are often excessive and 'blind' – their explanations are frequently based on a view of humans as cognitive and rational beings. The focus on rationality in the SIT tradition fails to adequately explain why groups, or we could say discursive practices of groups, manage to 'fix' subjects to themselves. In order to adequately answer the above three questions, we need to turn to the central instruments of subjectivity.

Conformity: from cognition to recognition

SCT presents social influence as a matter of self-categorization into a reference group, and a consequence of depersonalization. People who we perceive to be part of the ingroup category influence us. Hogg and McGarty summarize SCT's view of conformity:

> First, people categorize and define themselves as members of a distinct social category or assign themselves a social identity; second, they form

or learn the stereotypic norms of that category; and third, they assign these norms to themselves and thus their behavior becomes more normative as their category membership becomes salient.

(Hogg & McGarty, 1990, p. 15)

We can ask whether there is such a neat step-by-step procedure in social influence, and we can consider to what extent this statement paints an image of social influence as a voluntary act. But let us leave aside these issues and instead ask the following more basic question: does this account say anything about *why* people assign group norms to themselves? Turner et al. (1987) state that conformity "is believed to originate in the need of people to reach agreement with others perceived as ... psychological ingroup members" (p. 72). But *why* is there such a need? Why should the norms of the reference group have such influence on people? SCT is clear on the fact that we do not identify with or conform to groups simply because they offer solutions to problems that we cannot solve on our own. Although this may hold true in some cases, such practical explanations do not adequately explain why groups – or, more correctly, group ideals – manage to impose themselves on us. To answer the two preceding questions, an analysis of the historical, discursive and ideological context will not be enough. We need to take seriously a psychoanalytical factor of subjectivity: the factor of desire.

What does the group want from me?

From a psychoanalytic framework, we identify with group prototypes and ideals because we are searching to obtain the recognition and love of the reference group (or the symbolic Other). "It is in terms of ... want-to-please attitude or its corollary, a fear to displease (or what Lacan formulates as a primitive need for recognition and love)" (Alcorn, 2002, p. 40) that conformity to groups should be understood. The following statement by Alcorn offers an insight into components of group life that SCT fails to theorize:

> From early in our life, groups make demands of us to laugh with them, eat their food, appreciate their models of beauty, and feel repulsion towards things they despise. When our performance earns their approval, they smile at us with recognition. We show the first step in any kind of understanding; we understand what the Other wants.
>
> (Alcorn, 2002, p. 104)

The identities of group members are formed on the ego-ideals, or stereotypes, of the social category (i.e. the Other) in question. As Reicher et al. (2010) argue, "members will both actively seek out and respond to information about the nature of their group stereotype and its action implications" (p. 53). People 'seek out' what is expected of them from their groups, they attempt to understand what the group wants from them. In other words, they try to figure out the *desire of the Other*.

Desire is unfortunately missing in SCT (and in the SIT paradigm more generally). According to psychoanalysis, desire lies at the very heart of the human condition, and, we could say, at the centre of group processes. Without the notion of desire, we will not begin to understand how groups become salient, and how values and norms, the ego-ideals, of the group manage to impose themselves on individuals. One of the useful elements of the Lacanian School is that it has a dialectical conceptualization of desire. Desire is not a repressed longing deep within us, but something which always needs to be understood as a result of the attempt to live up to the ego-ideals of the Other, and to assume a symbolic identity pleasing to this Other. "The human experience of identity is constructed via identification with the signifiers of the desire of the [O]ther" (Vanheule & Verhaeghe, 2009, p. 399). The subject's existence is defined by the question 'what does the Other want from me?' With this question, he makes his own desire the desire of the other: 'I desire to be desired by the Other'. How we think that we are seen, how we understand ourselves, is possible by *recognizing* ourselves through the eyes (or the discourse) of the big Other. Social identification always comes with a fantasy that displays the desire of the reference group. "Fantasy answers the question of who and what I am to the [Other]" (Dean, 2006, p. 12). In a sense, the subject becomes what he unconsciously perceives that the reference group wants him/her to become; the subject's constant assumption is that the group knows the answer to who he or she is or should be, and therefore identifies with the desire of the Other. Let us spell out that it is ego-ideals that define the desire of the Other. Desire is therefore manipulated by the use of ego-ideals. It now becomes clearer how the group manages to direct action; it does so via desire and ego-ideals. We can therefore state that *ego-ideals both enable and inhibit action through desire*.

Group identification and influence is thus more a matter of desire for love and recognition than cognitive computations or perceptual processes. Freud's (1959) contribution to group psychology was exactly this claim – that the group is held together due to love identifications. It is an emotional quality that bonds people together in a group. In times of enhanced globalization, increased individualism and intense social conflict, this quality can turn into an excessive, and often destructive, affective attachment.

The group bond and enjoyment

For SCT, group cohesiveness, or the group bond, is a matter of cognition. "The most distinctive theoretical feature of the self-categorization analysis of group formation and cohesion is the idea that they depend upon the perception of self and others as a cognitive unit" (Turner et al., 1987, p. 64). The neglect of affect in the theorization of group unity has led Hogg and McGarty (1990) to state that "despite the affective nature of group membership and group solidarity social identity theory dwells little upon theoretical explication of 'hot' aspects of the group" (p. 20). Their argument is, however, that SCT offers a promising way to examine this affective element via its theory of attraction. Attraction to the group is viewed in terms of self-categorization and prototypicality. "How much individual group members are liked is ... a function of their perceived prototypicality" (p. 20). But does this actually say anything about the 'hot' aspects, the physicality, of the group? For Hogg and McGarty, the social 'glue' remains a matter of cognitive categorization. If we were to understand categories in terms of the signifier, we could, in some ways, accept that categorization is fundamental in producing group solidarity. The signifier does indeed play a determining role in binding different people together, but again, this does not say much about the affective nature of the group bond.

In his later work, Lacan moved away from a focus on the signifier and concentrated instead on something that animates discourse, yet cannot be totally represented in discourse. He began to pay more attention to the bodily and physical experiences of the subject that are not easily accommodated in the symbolic. He showed how these experiences motivate many of the subject's thoughts and actions. Later Lacanian theory highlights the affective aspects of identification often existing just beneath the level of conscious awareness (which is not to say that these aspects cannot also be conscious). One of the main factors that drive group identification processes is exactly this affective experience that escapes cognition, discourse and the symbolic:

> Focusing on the symbolic aspects of identity ... although a necessary step ... is not sufficient in order to reach a rigorous understanding of the drive behind identification acts, to explain why certain identifications prove to be more forceful and alluring than others, and to realize why none can be totally successful.
>
> (Stavrakakis, 2008, p. 1050)

So, what is this affective experience that neither the SIT paradigm nor the discursive perspective in social psychology pays attention to? This is a special kind of intense enjoyment, known as *jouissance*.

> *Enjoyment* (*jouissance*) refers to an excessive pleasure and pain, to that something extra that twists pleasure into a fascinating, even unbearable intensity ... it is a special kind of agony, an agony that makes us feel

more alive, more fully present, more in tune with what makes life worth living, and dying for, than anything else. Enjoyment, then, is this extra, this excess beyond the given, measurable, rational, and useful ... enjoyment is that 'something extra' for the sake of which we do what might otherwise seem irrational, counter productive, or even wrong.

(Dean, 2006, p. 4)

We can understand the affective bond to the group in terms of *jouissance* because "where there is affect, there is *jouissance*" (Fink, 1999, p. 212). This is a physical, a *bodily* factor. In Lacanian theory, human social constitution necessarily entails the *prohibition* of this *jouissance*. This prohibition "is exactly what permits the emergence of desire, a desire structured around the unending quest for the lost, impossible *jouissance*" (Stavrakakis, 2008, p. 1053). It is lost and impossible because we can never gain complete *jouissance*. We 'lack' because we are unable to ultimately attain a sense of full enjoyment: "when subjectivity is conceived in terms of lack ... this lack can be understood as a lack of *jouissance*" (Glynos & Stavrakakis, 2008, p. 261). Identification with ego-ideals of the group nevertheless conceals this fundamental lack. Through identification the subject tries to experience some of this 'lost' *jouissance*. Group members find enjoyment in bonding with one another, and in the very practices of duty and conformity. This possibility of enjoyment makes it very difficult to avoid influence, or indeed, to leave a group.

To be absolutely clear then we could state that *jouissance bonds people in a group*. The search for this bodily experience plays a powerful role in attracting people to groups. Especially in the contemporary world, characterized by fragmentation and increased individualism and uncertainty, groups that offer 'stability', a sense of unity, and the promise of full enjoyment tend to be very successful in pulling subjects to themselves. SCT researchers admit that the experience of uncertainty increases the need for group identifications, and often strengthens the group bond (e.g. Hogg, 2000). Most groups, whether religious, ethnic, work-based, web-based or based on sexual orientation, promise a fulfilled life, they promise *jouissance*, and since modern subjects long for fullness, they tend to submit themselves to these groups. In fact, modern individualist and consumerist societies, instead of doing away with communities have paradoxically increased the desire for groups and togetherness. Some examples of modern groups that are ever more crucial as the basis of identity are religious, national and even professional groups (as they can be, for example, a foundation for prestige and status). We can therefore not neglect the important role of *jouissance* in maintaining the "grip of identity" (Glynos & Stavrakakis, 2008, p. 266), because without this affective element, identity would not function, it would not be kept in place, and it would not stick. It is the reach for *jouissance* that makes us identify with political projects, social roles or consumer choices. In fact, *jouissance* can in itself function as a "purpose, a cause" (Stavrakakis, 2007, p. 183). *Jouissance*, or shared enjoyment, then, holds a group together; it is what bonds the community. How exactly does it manage to do this? For example, cultural rituals and ceremonies of a group, the specific myths and practices offer a common identity, but these also keep a fantasy in place, which includes a taste of *jouissance* in bonding with one another. Tajfel (1981) recognizes that the characteristics of a group are "value laden" (p. 277). This is so because certain practices, rituals and traditions including the zeal and the ardour present in some national practices (for example, celebrated sporting victories) are only material manifestations of *jouissance*. These characteristics of the group become signifiers of value, they represent group distinctiveness. Thus, not only does enjoyment bind people within a group, it also differentiates the group from other groups. The features of the group always gain value in relation to other groups, they are always relational, as they signify difference to other groups: they become the valued property, the 'Thing' of the group (Žižek, 1993). More specifically, "our Thing is our belief that these features make us who we are" (Dean, 2006, p. 14). We can also therefore state that the category prototype as that position which best differentiates the ingroup from the outgroup or, to be more exact, which maximizes inter-category differences compared to intra-category differences, can represent the 'Thing' which makes a group what it is. The Thing is the enjoyment in the practices, rituals and ideals of the group. What differentiates one group from another group is enjoyment: each group has its own idiosyncratic ways of enjoying. Žižek (1993) states in relation to national groups: "a nation *exists*, only as long as its specific enjoyment continues to be materialized in a set of social practices and transmitted through national myths or fantasies that secure these practices" (p. 202). We can therefore "consider the collapse, disintegration, or transformation of nations in terms of changes in their enjoyment. A community may no longer be a community when there is no belief in a shared enjoyment" (Dean, 2006, p. 14).

Although the SIT paradigm does emphasize differentiation and comparison as a fundamental group and intergroup process, it does not offer concepts to understand the passionate element of differentiation. Rather than fulfilling "the need that the individuals have to provide social meaning" (Tajfel, 1981, p. 276), differentiation preserves the particular ways in which a group gains its *jouissance*, and defends itself from the threat of the outgroup who wants to steal it or contaminate it with their own *jouissance*. Thus, a group is bonded by and gains *jouissance* from problematizing foreign, *other* modes of *jouissance*, which are simultaneously viewed as embodying the very kernel of alterity, otherness, and as threatening to given, existing modes and approaches to *jouissance*. A "community's enjoyment … come to the fore in myths and fantasies – myths that generally explain the ways our enjoyment is threatened by others who want to steal it, who want to ruin our way of life by corrupting it with their own peculiar enjoyment" (Dean, 2006, p. 15). We think that other groups enjoy more than us, or that they will contaminate us with their particular ways of enjoying, a mode of enjoyment that we cannot stand. "We hate their enjoyment and see them as foreign and threatening and thus acquire a sense of the special quality of *our* way of life. Our enjoyment becomes real to us as ours to the extent that we are already deprived of it" (Dean, 2006, p. 15).

Indeed, *jouissance* was already taken away from each one of us when we became social beings; we are already dispossessed. Ceremonies and practices of the group only offer a *partial* and *temporary* experience of *jouissance*, which to an extent explains why group rituals, practices and myths constantly have to be repeated. The momentary nature of *jouissance* will never fully satisfy desire. In other words, identification with group ideals will never offer a sense of final unity. The psychoanalytic subject will always remain a lacking subject. It is the search for (and partial experience of) *jouissance* that nevertheless creates a fantasy of identity, of community, of oneness. In fact we can even go so far as to say that complete identification with the group is an impossible *illusion*. Identity is ultimately a failure, which is why subjects never stop identifying with, for example, political or national discourses, continuously aiming to gain fullness once and for all. It is also an illusion because the imaginary similarity between individual members of the group is exactly just that: imaginary. The group constitutes an "imaginary collective identity … The imaginary integration of *what we are* … cover[s] up the real separation between individual subjects" (Pavón Cuéllar, 2010, p. 15). There is always considerable diversity within a group – for instance within one nation there are regional, linguistic and cultural differences – which are usually covered over with the invocation of one social category. There is nothing that bonds individuals together apart from a symbolic category (The 'Nation') and a series of practices (language, royal weddings) that embody shared enjoyment. Identity is therefore an illusion that nevertheless manages to have significant material effects on individuals and society.

Salience and enjoyment

The search for the bodily factor of enjoyment can also explain why some categories become more salient than others. In SCT, salience refers to the fact that "self-conception varies across levels of abstraction or relative inclusiveness. The salient level of abstraction determines the content of self-perception, which in turn determines the form of social behavior" (Oakes, 1987, p. 117). In any given situation, a specific group membership becomes cognitively important and has immediate influence on the thinking and action of the individual. This aspect of SCT depicts the social self-concept as fluent and situational. 'Accessibility' and 'fit' are the terms that explain the salience of categories. Those categories that will be used for self-definition are accessible in the specific situation. The concept of fit refers to the degree to which reality is perceived to reflect social category differences. Salient categories minimize intraclass differences compared to interclass differences. All this means that "as the world varies so does category salience. As the 'other' with whom we compare ourselves changes so does our 'self' ... categories have to be appropriate to the comparative context" (Reicher et al., 2010, p. 54).

If we put aside for a moment this account's depiction of the human being as a computer, we can admit that identities are often situational. To give an example, within a professional organization, we act according to the organization-wide norms in some contexts, and according to our specific departmental or team norms in other contexts. We could even interpret 'context' as the specific symbolic framework that imposes on us its discursive norms. There can be different instantiations of the symbolic, different authorities, or positions of knowledge that embody this function: we identify with different ego-ideals when we are working as a doctor at a hospital as opposed to when we are home with our children. Momentary, transient categories may be categories with little long-term impact, and indeed, the contemporary world largely consists of such identities. The problem is that although some idea of motivation is included in the 'accessibility' notion ("the person's current motives" help to determine accessibility of categories (Turner et al., 1987, p. 55)), SCT depicts salience in terms of cognition. Of course, we all belong to many different groups, some of which will be more salient than others in any given situation, but SCT underemphasizes, or overlooks, the way desire or affect can determine the salience of categories.

It is the desire for the bodily (and always temporary) experience of *jouissance* which is effectively involved in the salience of categories. To give an example, Stavrakakis (2007) claims that the reason why there is a failure to make salient a European hegemonic identity is because the project has been unsuccessful in evoking the necessary *jouissance* – the kind of emotional bond that exists in other forms of national identity. In fact, the *salient* category is the category that stands out, that becomes *sig*nificant for a subject; it becomes a *signifier*. We shall therefore note that despite being non-discursive, *jouissance* is always bound up with signifiers. As SCT researchers know well, categorization enhances the affective bond with other people. This points to the power of the signifier in conjuring up affect. The signifier and affect are then inextricably linked. The salience of categories such as 'British', 'Muslim' or 'socialist' cannot be understood without their simultaneous production of affect.

We have already questioned in Chapter 2 whether identities in the real world can be switched on and off in the manner described by SCT. There must be a general continuity throughout a given social group in terms of the presiding Other that precisely holds this grouping together as a society and as a collective defined by certain values or key signifiers. When we take enjoyment into account, it will become possible to see how some identities are not as flexible and fluid as SCT and some discursive perspectives assume. "Enjoyment is what fixes the subject in its place … we might … think of it as what sticks to the subject, as what the subject can never shake or escape" (Dean, 2006, p. 17). This rather clinical understanding of enjoyment can be understood in relation to our identification with groups. Groups impose on us a place, and we are fixed in our attempts to fully occupy and identify with this place. In fact, SCT understates the power that groups have over us. As we have already declared, the reference group as the Other is the dominant factor, it overrides the 'self'. It is in terms of enjoyment that we should understand the way in which reference groups manage to fasten us into a framework of domination.

The group bond and transgression

We have stated that those groups that promise *jouissance* will manage to attract subjects to themselves, and it is those groups that will become salient. We have also pointed out the powerful bonding factor of *jouissance*. But the group bond is in fact rather complicated and counter-intuitive. Group ideals and norms permit, enable and direct *jouissance*, but they also prohibit and forbid. The SIT paradigm does not recognize that "what sustains a community may be not simply a shared identification with an official ideal … but also identification with a common form of *transgression* (from which we procure enjoyment)" (Glynos, 2001, p. 9). *It is often the transgression of official group ideals and norms that holds the group together.* Practices that transgress group ideals can sometimes bind a community much more powerfully than those that conform to ideals. Indeed, transgressive practices often support group ideals and bind a community together because "the very failure of an ideal's realization may perpetuate it, extend its life so to speak" (Glynos, 2001, p. 10). Ideals are usually not subverted through transgressive practices. They enable the *jouissance* that comes with transgression, and are therefore sustained through transgression. "Transgression can provide the common link, the libidinal support that binds a collective together – our collective dirty secret" (Dean, 2006, p. 35). Transgression can come in many forms, such as in jokes, misbehaviour and even in excessive conformity to norms. Someone who over-identifies with a group ideal to the extent that he or she goes beyond the limits put by the ideal may experience some form of enjoyment. Jokes, ridicule and parody of an ideal "make possible the enjoyment of their transgression, which in turn sustains those very same ideals" (Glynos, 2003, p. 8). By making the social norms look absurd, ridicule allows a *momentary* suspension of the usual order of things. However, ridicule and other such transgressive practices – which for a time appear genuinely subversive inasmuch as they call the status quo into question, make the ideals seem arbitrary – in fact actively support the existing structure. This is so exactly because they allow for the experience of a temporary thrill of *jouissance*, but people then 'get back to work'; the normal order of things then continues as it was.

In the following quote, Freud discusses the totem meal and the way regular patterns of transgressive *jouissance* manage to bond subjects to groups:

> Each man is conscious that he is performing an act forbidden to the individual and justifiable only through the participation of the whole … every instinct is unfettered and there is a license for every kind of gratification. Here we have easy access to an understanding of the nature of festivals in general. A festival is a permitted, or rather, obligatory excess, a solemn breach of a prohibition … excess is of the essence of the festival; the festive feeling is produced by the liberty to do what is as a rule prohibited.
>
> (Freud, 1955, p. 140)

This quote illustrates clearly how various forms of transgressions are often permitted. Other examples are demonstrations and carnivals within modern liberal societies. These are forms of shared transgressions or protests that are authorized. They enable a temporary space for enjoyment, but very rarely do they properly subvert the dominant ideals and practices of a community.

Conclusion

The point of this chapter has been to introduce and point out those aspects of group identification that both SCT and the discourse analytical approach downplay or ignore. From our Lacanian perspective, conformity to groups would be impossible without the subject's desire to be recognized by the Other. From this perspective moreover, the bonding factor of groups would be understood in terms of enjoyment. Category salience may in some ways contain a cognitive process, but this is secondary to the fact that those categories that speak to our desire for *jouissance* will be the ones that succeed in attaching their ideals to us. This chapter also discussed how the group could be sustained and united by a common form of transgression. Group identification is a complex process and often at odds with common sense. From the perspective of SIT, it would be bizarre to state that transgressing group ideals or ideologies can be an effective way to maintain group solidarity. The themes of transgression and resistance will reappear in Chapters 6–8.

5 Another story of the minimal group paradigm

When researchers in the SIT tradition discuss and theorize the minimal group experiments, "the experimenter's power is left out of the theorization" (Henriques, 1984, p. 77). This chapter takes seriously this charge against SIT. It uses some of the Lacanian concepts introduced in the previous chapters to offer an alternative reading of the minimal group paradigm that highlights the decisive role of the experimenter. The minimal group experiments are often said to demonstrate the effects of social categorization on intergroup discrimination or ingroup bias. The overarching argument of this chapter is that we should rather understand these experiments as an exemplification of the way discourse can construct subjectivity. Or more precisely, the way the symbolic can *produce* a particular psychology and thereby behaviour. From this perspective, the minimal group studies show how the symbolic can designate identity via signifiers (i.e. categories). The results of the experiments should thus be understood as conditioned by the symbolic, via the discourse of the experimenter. This discourse can be viewed as the objective ground for the participants' behaviour.

The first minimal group experiments

The aim of the minimal group experiments was to see whether people would show loyalty to groups they were put into in an arbitrary or meaningless manner. In other words, the experiments were to find the baseline condition for identification with groups. In the Tajfel et al. (1971) study, for example, the researchers ask: "can the very act of social categorization, as far as it can be identified and isolated from other variables, lead – under certain conditions – to intergroup behaviour which discriminates against the outgroup and favours the ingroup?" (Tajfel et al., 1971, p. 151). A number of studies were conducted around the 1970s and many of these have been replicated in different forms and with different types of subject.[2] This chapter focuses mainly on the very first series of experiments (i.e. Billig & Tajfel, 1973; Tajfel, 1970; Tajfel et al., 1971).

Tajfel and his colleagues produced a situation where the subjects of the experiment could in no way relate to each other in terms of their individuality. The only way to relate to other people would be in terms of their group membership. The early experiments would typically run in the following way: The researchers would collect a group of boys who knew each other well from a school in Bristol in the laboratory to participate in the experiment. The boys would be asked to first carry out a simple task – for example, estimate the number of dots flashed onto a screen, or state their preferences for a number of paintings by the artists Klee and Kandinsky. They would then be told they would be divided into two groups based on the tasks they performed – for example, on their performance on the dot guesses or on their preferences for Klee or Kandinsky. They did not know that they were actually divided into the groups randomly. In the Billig and Tajfel (1973) experiment, however, subjects were allocated in an explicitly random manner into groups labelled 'X' and 'W'.

In the second part of the experiment, the subjects would be told that they would take part in another experiment, unrelated to the first, but the groups created in the first experiment would be used for this second experiment. They were then asked to allocate points, which would be exchanged for real money, to fellow subjects. They would be told to allocate points to two people who were both either from their own group, or from the other group. Sometimes the two people would be one from each group. The identity of the person they were giving the money to would not be known. They would only know which group this person belonged to. There would be no face-to-face or any other forms of interaction between the subjects within or between the groups. The only way the boys could relate to each other in this situation was therefore on the basis of a trivial common label, such as 'overestimator' or 'underestimator', 'Klee' or 'Kandinsky', 'X' or 'W'. They allocated the points alone in a cubicle by making choices on matrices. They were told they could not allocate money to themselves.

The boys' behaviour in these experiments indicated a rather 'irrational' attachment to their respective groups. Tajfel et al. (1971) noted that since the participants in the experiment knew each other, the most 'rational' strategy would have been one that awarded the ingroup, or at least distributed the money to everybody, but instead subjects chose to *differentiate* between their own group and the outgroup. In other words, they aimed to achieve positive differentiation in favour of their own social category, even at the cost of giving less money to the ingroup and the outgroup. The minimal group results are often used as evidence of the effect that an explicit social categorization (as opposed to situations with no such categorization) can have in producing ingroup favouritism and outgroup discrimination.[3]

As soon as the experimenters introduced the notion of categories, subjects would enhance and affirm this categorization process by differentiating their groups from other groups. This suggested to the researchers at the time that there is no need for face-to face interaction, interdependence or shared history between people, for the establishment of ingroup affiliation. It also confirmed that competition for scarce resources is not necessary for intergroup bias, as previously thought in social psychology.

The experiment and language

From the mainstream experimental perspective, the experiment is considered a scientific investigation into the nature of human behaviour. The assumption is that the experiment reveals something about group identification that was not known before. The only way to know, then, is through scientific scrutiny. The experiment is thus viewed as a method, a 'device' that will disclose the 'truth' about group belonging and intergroup relations. From the mainstream point of view, the experiment *itself* is not seen as an instance of group or even intergroup behaviour. Neither is it viewed as an example of the effects of human interaction and communication. What is more, "the empiricist division between experimenter and subjects is unquestioned" (Henriques, 1984, p. 77).

An experiment essentially consists of a series of communications between the experimenters and the participants in the experiment. *The experiment should be understood as a series of communicative acts.* There have been some attempts to explain the minimal group experiments in terms of a 'conversation logic' approach (Blank, 1997). According to this perspective, the result of ingroup favouritism is a function of the various communications within the experimental setting. The subjects would use the information about their groups because they assumed that this information must be relevant for the allocation task. This implies that the minimal group experiments (as all experiments) should be understood as a collection of linguistic or discursive interactions. However, this approach itself employs experiments to 'test' if the information about group membership has an impact on the allocation task. It does not see how an experiment, because it is an interaction between humans, is an instance of the workings of the symbolic, and more specifically, it does not take seriously the role of the experimenter in administrating this interaction.

In the early papers on minimal group studies, the authors point out the powerful impact of the experimenters' language on the subjects. For example, in discussing the results, Billig and Tajfel state:

> it seems that the mere mention of 'groups' by the experimenters was sufficient to produce strong intergroup discrimination. It was as if that,

just by inserting the word 'group' into the experimental instructions, the [subjects'] definition of the situation was radically altered. Standards or norms of behavior would seem therefore to inhere in the very concept of a 'group', and these norms were elicited by the explicit grouping of [subjects] in the minimal intergroup situation.

(Billig & Tajfel, 1973, p. 48)

From our Lacanian framework, a word, such as 'group', is an element of the symbolic, and it therefore carries with it and transmits, norms and expectations that are part of a wider socio-historical context. What is more, from this perspective, words, especially those that designate identity, have far-reaching consequences. "A discourse that is to move or even interest a subject must say, explicitly or implicitly, 'You are this,' or 'You are that'" (Bracher, 1993, p. 28). As we know from the previous chapters, words (read signifiers) only carry meaning in relation to other words. Indeed, as the minimal group researchers would argue, categorizing people in different groups, in other words the very act of *telling* people 'you are a member of this group', which of course implies 'you are not a member of the other group', has implications. A category is a label, and in the minimal group experiments the subjects were associated with other subjects by means of a common label, and they were dissociated from yet other subjects by means of a different label. A label – for example, 'Kandinsky' or 'X' – is an element of language, of the symbolic; it is a *signifier*. In the Billig and Tajfel (1973) study, the subjects where assigned to groups on an explicitly random basis, but these openly arbitrary criteria still offer a foundation for similarity for subjects. Members of the group 'X', for example, are similar in the sense that they all can identity with each other via the signifier 'X'. This signifier offers a point of identity, and similarity, even if the subjects never interact with each other in any form. Subjects in the category 'X' act more or less in a unitary manner (they tend to discriminate against, or differentiate themselves from, the 'W' group) because they are all under the influence of the same signifier 'X'. The similarity created between the various subjects in the category 'X' depends of course on the label 'X'. Thus, the word 'X' ascribes similarity between the members, despite the actual differences that may exist between them. In other words, from the perspective of the subject in the experiment, the only thing that connects him to other subjects is the signifier 'X', and the only thing that disconnects him from other subjects is a different signifier 'W'. Thus, 'X' can only *gain value in its difference* to 'W'. The minimal group experiments therefore demonstrated the effects of discourse, or from our Lacanian perspective, *they illustrated the impact of the symbolic.*

We may now ask ourselves a question with a very obvious answer: where do these signifiers 'X' and 'W' come from? Who introduces these signifiers in the setting? This is of course the experimenter. If we assume that subjects enter the experimental situation, consciously or unconsciously asking themselves 'what is required of me?' or 'what does the experimenter want from me?' (like the question that haunts all human beings: what does the Other want from me?), each step of the experiment, and each message of the experimenter, is interpreted by the participants as relevant to what is required of them. In other words, even beyond the official instructions given to them by the experimenters, subjects interpret what is 'really' required of them by reading the tacit messages of the experiment (the signifiers of the experiment). To be more precise, an experiment is based on a series of formal and informal instructions being communicated from the experimenter to those taking part in the experiment, who will assign meaning to these instructions. Given that it is the experimenter who designs and communicates the experimental procedure, we can state that the instructions, the communications, of the experimenter largely dictate the direction of the experiment. In fact, the relationship between the experimenter and the participants is fundamentally an unequal one: the task of the experimenter is to give instructions, and the participants are to obey these instructions. In the minimal group experiments the experimenter "represents authority" (Billig, 1973, p. 342). This signifying relationship between the experimenter and the subject, the scientist and the 'layperson', is glossed over in reports and discussions of the minimal group studies. It is often not mentioned, even though it structures and defines the entire experiment. Does all this mean that the results of the minimal group studies are nothing but an effect of subjects' conformity to the experimenter's demands?

The demand characteristics accusation

This has in fact been one of the more serious criticisms against the minimal group experiments (but a criticism which has not attracted enough attention). The argument here is that the specific setting of the experiment creates a 'demand characteristic' whereby the subjects are influenced by the experimenter's expectations (Gerard & Hoyt, 1974). The experiments did not necessarily demonstrate any 'real' attachment to the assigned groups. The subjects were implicitly encouraged to show ingroup favouritism, and they simply conformed to this expectation of the experimenter. Given that the group categorizations were made excessively salient in the allocation task, the subjects believed that the experimenter wanted them to use this information and discriminate against the outgroup. Advocates of the minimal group experiments have over the years made various claims against the demand characteristics argument. It is, for example, often said that Tajfel and his colleagues did not expect ingroup bias, they did not even intend to study intergroup discrimination but wanted to create a minimal condition for categorization (see Tajfel, 1974). However, this contradicts the early reports of the studies where it was clear the results were seen as an illustration of something that was already suspected by the researchers (Condor, 2003). Therefore, the expectations of the experimenters can certainly not be ruled out.

Psychologists within the mainstream approach have famously claimed that covert and unintended communication between the experimenter and the subjects often have a significant impact on the results of an experiment (Rosenthal, 1966). This idea is an example of the very many ideas in social psychology that have their roots in psychoanalysis (because they assume the existence of an unconscious). From a psychoanalytic perspective, even if the experimenters did not expect, or consciously intended to study intergroup discrimination, it would not be a satisfactory justification against the demand characteristics hypothesis, because experimenters may have had intentions that were not fully conscious. Psychoanalysis teaches us that any form of action or communication can have unintended consequences beyond the control of the acting or communicating subject. Experimenters may 'give off' messages which they do not intend, and which are the products of the language they are using, and the culture in which they are situated. From a Lacanian standpoint, the true meaning of any message is not found in the person who utters the message (for example, by asking them 'what did you really mean by that?') but in the way it is received by its audience, and in its consequences (in other words, it is the big Other that determines the meaning of a communicative act).

Returning to the critique against the minimal group experiments, St Claire and Turner (1982) conducted an experiment to investigate whether the demand characteristics allegation is valid. This is not the place to discuss the details of their experiment. What is crucial for our purposes is that the authors claim to show that the result of the minimal group experiments, the observed ingroup bias, is simply not a product of the specific experimental setting. Berkowitz (1994) is, however, not convinced. He claims to demonstrate that subjects clearly perceive that the experiment demands of them to favour their own group. In postexperimental reports, subjects stated that the group membership information and the categorization process gave hints about the experimenter's hypothesis. Harstone and Augoustinos (1995) also believe that demand characteristics cannot be excluded in the minimal group paradigm. They show that a three-group setting, rather than the standard two-group setting of the minimal group experiments, does not result in any significant ingroup bias. "There may be something particular about dichotomous categorization which elicits ingroup favouritism and outgroup discrimination" (pp. 188–189). A two-group context more clearly reflects group differentiations, and the situation would more easily be interpreted as 'us' versus 'them'. It is therefore not surprising that subjects demonstrated ingroup favouritism and outgroup discrimination in the minimal group studies. Harstone and Augoustinos (1995) argue that the results of these studies that used dichotomous groups "may reflect a culturally and linguistically based predisposition to respond competitively in such situations" (p. 191; see also Augoustinos and Walker, 1995, pp. 104–105). The authors argue that the absence of discrimination in a three-group situation resurrects the demand characteristics claim.

Although Tajfel (1978) does not accept the demand characteristics accusation, some of his writings indicate that his own interpretation of the minimal group experiments does not completely rule out the part that culture and language may have played in the minimal group studies. In a response to the demand characteristics hypothesis he states that if "what was no more than a hint from the experimenters about the notion of 'groups' ... had been sufficient to determine ... a *particular form* of intergroup behaviour" then we can assume that "this particular form of intergroup behaviour is one which is capable of being induced by the experimenters more easily than other forms (such as cooperation ...) ... at least in our culture" (p. 35). Tajfel also makes a note 'in parenthesis' about "the formation of a 'subjective' group membership amongst those who are lumped together as a group by others, even on the basis of generally inconsistent and varying criteria" (p. 37). It is not clear why this point should be made in parenthesis, as the argument about the powerful impact that outsiders have on creating a sense of ingroup unity reappears frequently in many of Tajfel's publications (see especially Tajfel, 1981, Chapters 11–15).

The primary role of the experimenter

In the minimal group studies, then, 'outsiders', who are the experimenters, have an immensely powerful role to play in creating not only a 'felt' group membership, as Tajfel argued, but also in influencing the results, as proposed by the demand characteristics hypothesis. The subjects were confronted with a situation in which the role of the experimenter was primary from the very beginning. They were *asked by the experimenter* to carry out a task, and then they were *separated by the experimenter* from everybody and were *asked* to allocate rewards to the other subjects. In the Tajfel et al. (1971) experiments, even though the subjects *believed* the experiments were conditioned by their judgments or preferences, it was the experimenter that created, introduced and imposed the categories on the subjects. In the Billig and Tajfel (1973) experiment, the experimenter's arbitrary construction of categories is made explicit to subjects. Indeed, Billig and Tajfel clearly define social categorization "as the explicit division of [subjects] *by the experimenters* into groups" (1973, p. 32, emphasis added).

We mentioned in previous chapters how easily people conform to and accept what comes from 'qualified' others, that is, those who are perceived to occupy a position of authority. "In the minimal group situation the experimenters create the group categories, and it has been found that [subjects] consistently accept the use of these categories" (Billig, 1973, p. 339). In other words, the subjects took on board the categories created by someone else (the experimenter) – 'Klee' or 'Kandinsky', 'X' or 'Y' – and assumed these categories as their own *without question*. These empty categorizations created by the experimenter became 'real' for the subjects. They identified with the categories they were allocated into despite the fact that these categories were very meaningless, and, as Tajfel (1981) states, "the 'empty' group condition in the experiment ... illustrates the *reductio ad absurdum* of this process" (p. 237).

The function of language is primary here. In the task which consisted of judging dots, for example, "the [subjects] *were told* by [the experimenter] that in judgements of this kind some people consistently tend to overestimate the numbers of dots projected and some consistently to underestimate them" (Tajfel et al., 1971, p. 155, emphasis added). This is a perfect example of how a structure of differentiation can be created by the *discourse* of the experimenter. The experimenter implicates the subjects into a logic of symbolic difference, and as we know from psychoanalysis "the symbolic hypothetically determines the same thing that it signifies" (Pavón Cuéllar, 2010, p. 20). In other words, the symbolic has serious implications: it determines behaviour.

We can now begin to see how it may not be so surprising that subjects' behaviour in the experiments demonstrated differentiation. As Henriques states:

> It is not unreasonable to suppose that subjects, if they continued to co-operate with the rules of the experiment at all, were left with no option but to make ... discriminations. Positive and negative evaluations were required by the methodology. The power of the experimenter to make the rules governing subjects' behaviour resides partly in the more general authority relations ... it resides in the unrecognized power of formulating a procedure which limits the possibilities of response.
>
> (Henriques, 1984, p. 77)

When explaining the behaviour of the boys, Billig and Tajfel (1973) dismiss the earlier 'social norms' account (as expressed in Tajfel et al., 1971), and instead point out the need for social identity, or more precisely, "the individual's need to define and place himself in the social world" (p. 50). Despite the fact that the authors acknowledge the influence of the words used by the experimenter, this explanation of the results focuses on the individual who took part in the experiment, it assumes that there must be something *in* the individual that is responsible for the behaviour manifested in the experiments. This analysis completely disregards the *situation* of the experiment and the experimenter's role. Therefore, paradoxically, although the minimal group experiments would show the powerful role of the 'group' in determining individual behaviour, and although Tajfel was critical of the ideology of individualism within social psychology, the individual is ultimately seen as the agent and the driving force behind social phenomena. This interpretation of the results has been criticized (e.g. Condor, 2003; Wetherell, 1996a, see also Chapter 2), even by researchers working with the experimental approach. For example, Hertel and Kerr (2001) contest the 'need for identity' argument and highlight instead the impact of social norms, or 'normative scripts', transmitted largely through words, that offer prescriptions for intergroup behaviour in a specific situation (also recall from the previous chapter Wetherell's (1982) research showing that intergroup discrimination cannot be found in all cultures).

We cannot, however, totally dismiss the claim about the need for psychological distinctiveness, differentiation, or indeed, the need for a distinctive social identity. Just by glancing at some contemporary examples of intergroup relations outside the laboratory, we find many cases where groups (and individuals for that matter) attempt to distinguish themselves. Many national, religious and ethnic groups, for example, often attempt to enhance their difference. But even if intergroup behaviour may sometimes be an effect of the 'need' for psychological distinctiveness, it is not something that can be assumed in advance. As we have emphasized, each group or intergroup relation must be analysed separately within its specific socio-historical and political context. In the context of the minimal group studies, however, we cannot overlook the fact that this 'need for distinctiveness' may have been created by the discourse of the experimenter when they explicitly distinguished participants by categorizing them into two separate groups. The *experimenter's discourse constructed differentiations using signifiers*. The minimal group experiments provided subjects with a specific symbolic position, such as 'X' or 'W'. The experiment conveyed to the subjects the message "You are an X", which is of course the same as saying "You are not a W". Given that it was the experimenter's discourse that introduced differentiations in the situation, the subsequent differentiations made by subjects between their own group and the outgroup could therefore be seen as conforming to the demand, or, we could state from our Lacanian perspective, the *desire* of the experimenter. Therefore, the 'need' for psychological distinctiveness is the 'need' for recognition or approval from the experimenter. After all, being distinctive means being seen as unique in the eyes of someone else. It is possible that the desire to be distinctive or to obtain approval from the experimenter (combined with a competitive social norm existing in Western societies) produced the behaviour we have witnessed in the minimal group studies. We should, however, not neglect the crucial fact that the obedience to the experimenter, the importance that is ascribed to his or her position, is *itself* a product of the wider normative structure of Western liberal societies. In these types of societies science and scientific activity are very much valued and cherished. People generally think highly of those who dedicate their lives to scientific work. In the psychological laboratory, the experimenter is seen as the agent of science, and "supreme knowledge [is] projected onto the person of the experimenter" (Stavrakakis, 2008, p. 1051). It would therefore not be totally unreasonable to assume that the experimenter within the minimal group studies was ascribed a position of authority and respect. The experimenter becomes the 'subject supposed to know', and we can assume that the relation between the subject and the experimenter is an affective one. Subjects' attachment to their designated categories reflects a deeper emotional attachment to the experimenter. This is evidenced by the participants' tendency to accept the categories of the experimenter without question.

The experiment as an instance of inter- or intragroup relation

This interpretation of the minimal group situation allows us to see how there are, in this situation, three groups present: two groups consisting of participants in the experiment, plus another group consisting of the experimenters. The individuals in the two 'participant' groups are very similar. In the case of the early classic studies, they are all similar-aged schoolboys from the same school. They are all also considered 'participants in an experiment'. So, even if they are divided into two distinct groups by the experimenter, there is not much that differentiates the boys across the groups; they are essentially very similar in this context. However, the group consisting of the experimenters (and possibly their assistants and colleagues) radically differs from the group of schoolboys. The individuals in this group are not 'participants' in the experiment; they are 'experimenters', 'scientists', 'psychologists' or whatever else they may have called themselves. They play a radically different role within the experiments. They are therefore radically Other to the schoolboys. They are the symbolic Other because, as we know from previous chapters, the symbolic – just like the experimenter in the minimal group paradigm – offers the subject a sense of being. We stated above that subjects are faced with an unfamiliar situation that creates uncertainty (which could very well turn into anxiety). The schoolboys enter the experimental situation not knowing what is expected of them: they lack knowledge of what they are supposed to do and who they are supposed to be in this particular situation. This would be a good example of an occasion where the 'lack' of the subject is made particularly present. It is therefore not surprising that they would invest in the categories of the experimenter, because the categories provide a sense of being in a situation were they lack being. The symbolic categories of the experimenter offer knowledge, a sense of imaginary fullness. This idea is not dissimilar to the SIT tradition's 'subjective uncertainty' hypothesis. But subjective uncertainty should be understood in terms of the fundamental and eternal 'lack' of the subject, an emptiness that creates an unending desire for a sense of completion. Moreover, in the context of the minimal group experiments, the subjective uncertainty hypothesis could help to point out the role that the categories play in reducing this uncertainty, but it would underestimate the role of the experimenter.

The present chapter's reinterpretation of the minimal group studies implies that the experiment itself can be understood in terms of the imaginary and the symbolic discussed in Chapter 3. The experiment consists of a group with imaginary and symbolic elements. The relations between the groups of schoolboys are imaginary relations, and the relation between the group of schoolboys and the group of experimenters are symbolic relations (in this sense, rather than an instance of intergroup relations, we could even interpret the minimal group studies as an example of intragroup relations). The group of experimenters become the 'reference group', or, from our Lacanian perspective, they become the big Other. The subjects view themselves from the perspective of the big Other, and conform to the Other's demands. For that reason, the minimal group studies did not only demonstrate subjects' identification with their assigned social categories; they also showed the more primary, and more powerful, identification with the perspective of the experimenter (i.e. the big Other). In the experimental situation, therefore, the experimenter as the symbolic big Other determines the subject and his or her behaviour. The minimal group experiments are in fact a useful metaphor for the 'external' production of the subject, the fact that the subject is produced via identification with something Other to him or herself. As Tajfel points out, the experiments show "a correspondence between the experimenter's external criteria and the subject's internal criteria guiding their behaviour" (Tajfel, 1981, p. 234). We could say the 'internal' of the subject is a product of something 'external'. Lacanian theory emphasizes that what is most 'interior' to us is located elsewhere; it is an effect of something 'exterior' (see Pavón Cuéllar, 2010). The subjects in the experiment 'take on' the external categories, and assume them as their own, and in behaving in terms of these categories, they affirm and reproduce them: in favouring these categories in the allocation task, the subjects become the 'agent' of these categories. So, from this perspective, the subjects of the experiments are not exactly equal to the 'flesh and blood' human beings that actually participated in the experiments. Given that they were the *creation* of the experimenters discourse, they are merely signifiers, acting on behalf of another signifier: 'the experimenter'.

Conclusion

This chapter has reworked the minimal group paradigm with the help of some Lacanian theoretical concepts. The early experiments were read as illustrations of the operation of the symbolic, and, in particular, of the functioning of the experimenter as an embodiment of the big Other. From this perspective, more than anything else, the experiments demonstrated the function of the symbolic in the psychology of humans.

We have to bear in mind that this translation of the experiments is just *our interpretation* (more correctly, *my* interpretation) of the minimal group paradigm, just like the 'results' of the early experiments, and the subsequent development of the SIT, were little else than Tajfel and his colleagues' interpretation of what happened to the schoolboys in the experiments. This is exactly what Lacanian theory teaches us as researchers: that our understanding of the world is only *our* imaginary construction of it; it is never the world *itself*. Tajfel and his colleagues designed the experiments, and invited a group of schoolboys into the laboratory and asked them to carry out a series of tasks. We can only *guess* what *actually* happened to these boys (how they felt, how they understood the situation, what made them decide who to allocate the points to, etc). The statistical manipulations by Tajfel and his colleagues were little else than tools helping the researchers to *construct* a story of what happened. This story can of course be challenged, and it certainly has been over the years by other researchers, who have offered their own interpretations, their own stories. Each researcher can emerge with new experiments, and new constructions, trying to explain something not yet explained. Each new explanation will leave a gap: researchers can forever attempt to capture something that always tends to escape complete understanding of group behaviour, but scientific discourse will never be capable of encapsulating the full complexity and unpredictability of such behaviour. Indeed, we can even go so far to say that scientific discourse rather than *explaining* 'group behaviour' often ends up *constructing* it.

6 Social change or socio-symbolic symptom?

The emphasis on social change has been lost – if not repressed – in the very burgeoning field of 'social identity' research.

(Reicher, 1996, p. 318)

Categories of, for example, religion, class or occupation, stand in power and status relations to one another. The SIT tradition, at least as Tajfel developed it, is chiefly concerned with the relations between such large-scale social categories, and, in particular, with collective action and social movements. Following Tajfel (1981), we could define the latter as group actions that have specific aims with regard to the outgroup:

In the most general ways, these aims must include either changing the nature of the intergroup situation in conflict with groups wishing to maintain the *status quo*, or maintaining the intergroup *status quo* in conflict with groups wishing to change it.

(Tajfel, 1981, p. 291)

The SIT paradigm offers a social psychological account of social stability and change. Although objective and contextual factors are taken to play a significant role in determining the extent to which change is possible, SIT nevertheless highlights the *subjective* effects of these factors: the extent to which relations between groups are subjectively perceived as legitimate and stable will determine if or how people will attempt to sustain or alter the status quo. This chapter puts into question the understanding of 'subjective' as equal to 'perception'. Chapter 2 pointed out the SIT paradigm's over-emphasis on cognitive processes, and its over-reliance on the image of the rational subject. Social change and stability are understood largely as a result of cognitive mechanisms, as a matter of perception, judgement and reasoning. What is more, some ideas in the SIT paradigm are based on the neoliberal illusion that individuals have predictable beliefs, and will naturally act in their best interest to improve their lives and further their goals. Our desire for a positive social identity is assumed to trigger action whenever the circumstances allow, and those with 'negative' identities will attempt to refashion their identities. In some ways, in the 'social creativity' idea – despite being understood as a non-individualistic strategy – there is a glimpse of the liberal image of life as a project of self-development, a site for creativity and the manufacture of a strong and lovable ego.

The main argument of this chapter is that social change and stability primarily concern questions of *affect*, and not cognition. Using concepts such as fantasy, desire, death drive and *jouissance*, the chapter challenges SIT's assumption that subordinated groups will engage in actions in order to further their interests and enhance their identities whenever they can. This chapter also underscores the ambivalent nature of social change strategies, and the relation of the latter to the desire of the symbolic Other. The points made in this chapter raise a question: can we classify certain group actions – such as riots or terrorism – as 'social change', or would they, in some cases, be better understood as socio-symbolic symptoms?

From individual mobility to collective struggle

One of the constituent assumptions of the SIT tradition is that since people strive for a positive social identity, being a member of a group that is denigrated, stigmatized or considered 'inferior' will create a tension. These group members do not, however, need to accept a subordinated identity. If the group does not confer positive distinctiveness, the members will attempt to do something about that, and what exactly they will choose to do depends on certain 'objective' social, economic and historical conditions. These conditions tend to produce specific psychological dispositions, or *subjective belief structures*. That is, the "individuals' belief systems about the nature and the structure of the relations between social groups in their society" (Tajfel & Turner, 1986, p. 9). Members can change their subordinated position by acting in terms of the 'self', either by physically (or psychologically) moving from the group, or they can act in terms of the group by staying in the group and collectively working for change. The latter strategy reflects a *social change* belief system, and the former a *social mobility* belief system.

The fantasy of social mobility

SIT suggests that if the group does not make a positive contribution to a person's social identity, the individual will attempt to physically or psychologically dissociate themselves from the group. Whenever the social system is believed to be flexible (group boundaries are not perceived as fixed and

closed, but open and permeable) the *social mobility* belief system is prevalent. The perception of society is one in which free movement of people
from one group to another is possible. This includes the assumption that
people can *individually* improve their social situation or status; it implies an
individualistic approach to change.

As Hogg and Abrams (1988) recognize, belief structure "does not necessarily have to coincide with the 'true' nature of society" (p. 27). The system
may thus be inflexible and closed, yet people may believe that individually
moving to more privileged and highly esteemed groups is possible. Hogg
and Abrams call this "the 'myth' of individual freedom". They use the term
myth "because individual mobility is not easy to accomplish, it is in fact
extremely difficult to successfully 'pass' from subordinate to dominant
group" (p. 28). Indeed, social mobility is never a complete 'exit' from the
previous group. SIT researchers often recognize that, more often than not,
when moving from one group to another, the signs of the previous group
persist. In societies where skin and hair colour are decisive markers of one's
position in the social structure, 'passing' becomes very difficult. Those who
do manage to improve their social status despite their skin colour, in actual
fact experience their existence at the 'border'. This is even the case for
individuals whose original group membership is not so visibly marked.
For example, people who 'objectively' (or economically) move from
being a member of the working class to a member of the middle class are
often haunted psychologically by their abandoned, or 'other', working class
identities: "the Othered position continually threatens to intrude"
(Walkerdine, 2006, p. 18). This does raise a question, with regard to SIT,
as to whether true social mobility even exists. If people who appear to cross
group boundaries remain – psychologically (and even materially, as evidenced by the example of women in top corporate positions earning less than
their male counterparts) – at the 'borders', then we can ask whether there
actually is such a thing as 'true' exit from a group.

The reality (and in some cases the knowledge) that true social mobility
may not actually exist does not weaken the *belief* in social mobility. This
belief, characteristic of Western liberal cultures, but also prevalent in non-
Western societies, masks the inflexibility of the system and the reality that
people in subordinated groups have very little opportunity to move from one
group to another. The very few who manage to change and improve their
status are often used as examples in order to maintain the illusion that
'everybody can make it'. This keeps the unequal power structure intact
and change is inhibited: "By allowing some 'passing', the high-status
group provides evidence that it is doing something for members of the
unprivileged group. Consequently, larger-scale efforts can be avoided"
(Chryssochoou, 2004, p. 22). One question that the SIT tradition offers no

satisfactory answer to is the following: exactly *how* does the social mobility belief structure function to loosen the cohesiveness of subordinated groups and direct attention away from collective action? In order to answer this question we need to take seriously the 'myth' element of social mobility. We could think of 'myth' as a euphemism for 'fantasy'. *The social mobility belief structure is in fact a fantasy.* It is the fantasy quality of this belief system that manages to reproduce inequality and discourage collective challenge to the status quo. The fantasy of social mobility sustains the illusion that everybody has equal opportunity to improve their life conditions and status, and increase their wealth. It is based on an image of ourselves and others as "liberal, free, and self-relating human beings to whom multiple choices are open and all can be accommodated" (Contu, 2008, p. 370). This fantasy – which is often sustained in discursive and cultural practices, in Hollywood movies and self-help books, for example – is very effective in reproducing the existing system of power, as it *maintains* people in a position of 'trying to make it', and attention is directed away from collective struggle.

The Lacanian definition of fantasy takes seriously this aspect of fixity in a position of 'trying'. Fantasy in Lacan "provides a schema according to which certain positive objects in reality can function as objects of desire" (Žižek, 1997, p. 7). The nature of fantasy is such that it is most prominent when the subject is faced with an impossible situation, a feeling that something is missing or lacking, which arises from the desire to attain that which is missing and gain fullness. The purpose is, however, not to satisfy desire. "Rather, fantasy's primary aim is to *sustain* the subjects' desire by telling it *how* to desire" (Glynos, 2001, p. 200). The fantasy of social mobility upholds the desire for wealth and property, for example. Failure will only function to reproduce the desire; it will mean that people will keep trying, instead of questioning the very system that keeps them in that position. Fantasy therefore has a *"stabilizing* function … it *sustains* the subject as a *desiring* subject by providing it with a way of enjoying, a mode of *jouissance. Jouissance* is the enjoyment a subject experiences in sustaining his or her desire" (Glynos, 2001, p. 201). Merely desiring something (and not necessarily getting it) offers some kind of enjoyment to the subject. We should therefore not underestimate the power of *jouissance* in maintaining the fantasy of social mobility and preventing collective action. This does of course mean that fantasy is not exactly opposite to reality, because it works to *structure* social reality. It functions exactly to construct, as well as to maintain, an unequal social world. We shall also note that in social mobility, people never actually act as individuals. Indeed, as Hogg and Abrams (1988) recognize, "subjective belief structures reflect the predominant ideology" (p. 27). If there is a sociality in each and every individual, it follows that even when people try to change their situation by acting individually, they are under the influence of a certain social and cultural ideology, a big Other, that emphasizes individual mobility and success over collective struggle. In other words, the ideology of individualism so prevalent in many of today's societies is a *social* representation (see Farr, 1996). The social mobility belief system, representing the predominant ideology, and therefore inhibiting change, is in SIT opposed to the social change belief system. However, according to the theory, for the social change belief system to prevail there need to exist *cognitive alternatives* to the existing relations between the various groups.

Cognitive alternatives and the lack in the symbolic

The social change system of belief is likely to hold when it is difficult for individuals to objectively or psychologically move from one group to another, and when the social system constitutes a rigid hierarchical arrangement of groups in divisions of power. SIT predicts that in these situations individuals will stay in their groups and act collectively to change the stigma attached to their identities, and/or alter their subordinated social position. However, why is it that a situation of impermeable group boundaries, and a clear-cut division between groups in wealth and power does not always lead to the social change belief system? Why is it that those with stigmatized and subordinated identities do not always strive for positive differentiation? SIT theorists recognize that a "negative social identity is not sufficient condition for seeking positive group distinctiveness with respect to the high status ... outgroup" (Turner & Brown, 1978, p. 205). Conditions that will most likely *not* lead to social action are:

- weak prohibitions to individual movement from one group to the other, which will reduce the unity of the subordinated group;
- social comparison with other subordinate groups rather than with the dominant group, which will lessen the salience of the subordinate–dominant group conflict;
- the absence of cognitive alternatives (Tajfel & Turner, 1986).

Beyond 'objective' constraints, the latter is seen as the most important factor that determines whether or not groups will engage in social action to change their subordinated position. The existence of a social change belief system thus depends on whether or not there is awareness within the group that the existing social system is not the only possible one. A 'stable' or 'secure' social identity reflects a situation where there is consensus about the existing relations between groups, and no awareness of alternatives. In societies structured by a rigid caste system, for example, a change in the relations between the different castes is often not conceivable and social identity is therefore secure. This is the situation where a different system is not psychologically conceivable.

What brings about cognitive alternatives? Tajfel (1981) argues that what must first and foremost take place is "the breaking down of the barriers preventing the group from obtaining improved access to conditions which it could not previously obtain" (p. 284). In today's globalized world, this would include, for example, access to education and some form of media technology. Turner and Brown (1978) identify two factors that contribute to the development of cognitive alternatives:

1 *perceived instability*, which is the "groups' perception that their respective status positions can be changed";
2 *perceived illegitimacy*, which is defined as "the degree to which the groups perceive their status relations to conflict with superordinate values of justice, fairness or equity" (p. 209).

This implies that perceived instability *per se* does not necessarily lead to a search for positive distinctiveness, if the group's inferior position is perceived to be legitimate. When a specific social structure is no longer seen to be legitimate, the group will compare themselves with outgroups (even with groups that are radically different to one's own group) and this comparison can become an important force for intergroup behaviour and social action: "the perceived illegitimacy of an intergroup relationship is ... socially and psychologically the accepted and acceptable lever for social action and social change in intergroup behaviour" (Tajfel, 1981, p. 267). The opposite is also true: perceived illegitimacy of a group's inferior position does not necessarily lead to social action if the social system is perceived to be stable – that is, that it cannot be changed. "Providing that individual mobility is unavailable or undesirable, consensual inferiority will be rejected most rapidly when the situation is perceived as both unstable and illegitimate" (Tajfel & Turner, 1986, p. 22). In order for power to reproduce and maintain itself, subordinated groups will thus need to be deprived of certain material conditions and possibilities, and there needs to be an absence of cognitive alternatives, that is, the social system should be perceived as stable and legitimate. In explaining the factors that inhibit social or collective action, SIT highlights therefore the material and social relations between groups (for example, the rigidity of group boundaries, access to education), which will influence subordinated groups' *perception* of change and stability.

The notion of cognitive alternatives is not something completely new or original. In other disciplines, such as political theory, it is associated with the concept of *ideology*. Ideology is in this field understood as produced by social and discursive practices that make possible certain viewpoints and actions, and limits, or 'closes off', alternative ways of seeing and acting in the world. From this perspective "ideology always presents itself as something which is locked into a logic of necessity ('there is no alternative', etc.) which cannot, or at least should not, be tampered with or deviated from" (Daly, 1999, p. 222). Unequal relations between groups are then maintained when an ideology presents the prevailing social order as the only possibility. Lacanian theorists of ideology would understand what SIT calls 'the system' (or the 'belief system') in terms of the symbolic system. *It is the symbolic system that creates the signifying social relations between groups.* The symbolic is therefore in many ways equal to the *material*. It conditions the objective social structure, and the material boundaries between social categories.

SIT is right when, in its theory of social change, it highlights the importance of *belief*. As noted in Chapter 3, it is the subject's belief in the symbolic system that upholds the latter, but as we already know, belief is not sustained through cognition alone:

> Symbolic power presupposes a particular type of relation between those who exercise the power and those who are subjected to it, a relation of *belief* which results in complicity. Such a belief cannot be cultivated and sustained without the mobilization and manipulation of affect and enjoyment.
>
> (Stavrakakis, 2007, p. 177)

The *elimination* of cognitive alternatives requires therefore the work of *fantasy* which functions to structure the subject's desire and *sense of reality*, and represents for the subject a world which is coherent and meaningful. Fantasy works to conceal alternatives; it is difficult for the subject to realize that there are alternatives to the prevailing order because it would mean a complete disintegration of the subject's reality; "a feeling of a 'loss of reality'" (Glynos, 2001, p. 201). Subjects are attached to the socio-symbolic network, not least because it guarantees the very identity of the subject, including the way in which he or she gains *jouissance*. Therefore, "to lose [these networks] would be like losing the world" (Contu, 2008, p. 374). Ideology that presents itself as the only alternative could not be sustained without working both on the symbolic and on the bodily dimension of *jouissance*.

How can we then understand the situations when belief in the system begins to wane and cognitive alternatives come into existence? Tajfel states that

> the building up of 'cognitive alternatives' to what appears as unshakeable social reality must depend upon the conviction, growing at least

amongst some members of the minority, that some cracks are visible in the edifice of impenetrable social layers, and that therefore the time has come to push *as a group*.

(Tajfel, 1981, p. 319)

The 'cracks' in the system should be understood in terms of the 'lack in the symbolic'. In Lacanian theory, not only is the subject a 'lacking' subject (which implies in this case a subject who is not unitary, and is haunted by a sense of incompleteness), but the symbolic is also theorized as lacking. The symbolic, the institutional and discursive network of a given society, is not 'closed', complete, perfect, and it is not the best, or most just, social order available (even though it often gives the impression that it is). On the contrary, it is incoherent, inconsistent, imperfect, and it is penetrable. The fact that the symbolic big Other is itself lacking is what makes resistance and change possible and this is the reason why subjects are never fully determined by discourse or power (Hook, 2008a; Stavrakakis, 2008). A significant step towards change is when members of a society begin to 'see' the lack in the symbolic, when they begin to realize that 'things could be different'. This is the same as saying that the social order is perceived as illegitimate and unstable.

Is the existence of cognitive alternatives enough?

As Tajfel (1981, p. 329) recognized, media and communications technology help to bring about cognitive alternatives, or, we could say, the realization that the symbolic is lacking. What we learn from Lacanian theorists of ideology, however, is that the existence of cognitive alternatives is *not* enough for people to alter their behaviours and engage in collective action for change: *cognitive alternatives do not displace symbolic identifications that are based on jouissance*. What is problematic in SIT is the definition of stability as something to do with the *perception* that the social order cannot change. The symbolic system, as implied above, structures subjects' fantasy, which in turn structures desire. A stable social system, even if perceived as changeable and illegitimate at a *cognitive* level, manages to evoke desire and keep desire alive: stability is a matter of desire, fantasy and affect, not cognition and perception. One can *know* that the system is illegitimate and that it can be changed, yet not *desire* change. Thus, beyond the perception of the possibility of change and the illegitimacy of the system, *what keeps the system intact and stable is desire*. Bracher (1993) makes this point very clearly when he states "if culture [including literature, communication technology, and any other medium that produces and distributes discourse] plays a role in social change, or in resistance to change, it does so largely by means of desire" (p. 19). It is not cognition or knowledge that keeps people in a certain social position or induces people to change their position: it is desire. The SIT tradition does not take seriously this rather obvious fact: in order to engage in struggles for change, people will need to *desire* change (see Stavrakakis, 2007).

One of the ways in which the symbolic system works to maintain desire is through its – explicit and implicit, official and unofficial – laws and regulations. As we stated in Chapter 4, there is a link between transgression and *jouissance*. The symbolic, or the laws of a given society, paradoxically both prohibits and permits *jouissance*. From a psychoanalytic perspective, there is no absolute distinction between law and the breaking of the law: the law itself is founded upon the possibility of its transgression. We stated in Chapter 4 that a community is often sustained by the transgression of its laws. Thus, by allowing some transgression, and the *jouissance* that comes with it, the social system can maintain desire and ultimately prohibit change. This is particularly so in many authoritarian societies where strict rules and laws on, for example, codes of conduct, are often transgressed, but this only functions to stabilize the system. (In some cases, the authoritarian state itself, in not-so-secret ways, encourages the very practices that it officially prohibits). To summarize our argument, a system is stable when it manages to sustain desire for *jouissance*. A stable symbolic system "relies on a libidinal, affective support that binds subjects to the conditions of their symbolic subordination" (Stavrakakis, 2007, p. 178). The socio-symbolic system's ability to offer temporary experience of *jouissance* inhibits desire for change: one does not easily give up *jouissance*.

Let us give an example. Tajfel discusses the case of some 'self-segregated' communities with cultures and values that deviate from the general norms of a society. He claims that the identity of the members of these groups is not necessarily 'threatened': there are 'deviant' groups that have their own "strongly integrated norms, traditions, values and function … One can remain happy and contented inside a ghetto, as long as this ghetto has not become socially disintegrated" (Tajfel, 1981, p. 327). For Tajfel, therefore, it is the strong integration of these communities that prevents them from developing cognitive alternatives and wishing to change their situation. What Tajfel under-emphasizes here is the fact that these groups' very existence is based on their deviance from the 'wider community system of norms'. Tajfel (1981) himself argues, "differentiation from others is, *by definition*, a comparison with others" (p. 337). Being 'deviant', or different, implies deviating from *something*, it implies being different from something. From our psychoanalytic point of view, being 'deviant' implies transgressing dominant and widely accepted socio-cultural laws and ideals (i.e. the symbolic). We know that transgression is never the exclusion or elimination of these laws. On the contrary, without transgression, there would be no laws. Transgression works to produce and uphold laws. We also know that transgression involves *jouissance*. We can therefore rework Tajfel's comment and state that *one can remain happy in a ghetto as long as it offers the possibility of jouissance*. From a SIT mode of reasoning, however, it would be difficult to see how an inferior, subordinated and deviant identity can be enjoyed, even if it is not consciously experienced as such. This is partly because SIT theorists adopt a simplistic or conscious understanding of 'pleasure' or 'satisfaction'. For example, when discussing the issue of social mobility, Tajfel considers the conditions that oblige people to remain in their groups:

> an individual will tend to remain a member of a group and seek member-
> ship of new groups if these groups have some contribution to make to
> the positive aspects of his social identity; i.e. to those aspects of it from
> which he derives some satisfaction.

> (Tajfel, 1981, p. 256)

If this requirement is not met, the individual will leave it unless it is 'objectively' impossible, or unless it "conflicts with values that are them-selves part of his acceptable self-image" (Tajfel, 1981, p. 64). Members from a subordinated group may indeed distance themselves from their 'inferior' community and identify instead with 'positive' ideals, which should be understood as the ideals of the Other (this implies social mobility, which, as we stated above, is ultimately an impossibility). Members can, however, also do the opposite: they can stay in a group that is consciously 'unsatisfactory', but that offers some form of unconscious enjoyment. The understanding of 'satisfaction' in Tajfel's above statement is one that equates to pure pleasure. This is very different from the Lacanian notion of *jouissance*, which is a bodily affect that involves a mixture of pleasure and non-pleasure. A sub-ordinated identity may be unsatisfactory both in the sense that it deprives members from material privilege, and in the sense that it is considered 'inferior'. Yet members can 'secretly' derive *jouissance* from belonging to a group that transgresses the ideals of the Other. In such cases, despite being seen negatively from the 'outside', the group has managed to promise or offer *jouissance* for its members. To reiterate, people can gain enjoyment from being a member of a 'subordinate' group even though this membership may not be 'satisfactory' in the conventional sense of the term.

The system's reliance on fantasy, desire and *jouissance* in stabilizing itself, the fact that subjects are deeply attached to the socio-symbolic struc-ture in which they find themselves, implies that social change struggles often become an ambivalent endeavour. It means that social creativity strategies, which may seem on the surface to be based on the existence of cognitive alternatives and a social change belief structure, can demonstrate a hidden unrelenting attachment to the symbolic big Other.

Social change strategies

In SIT, the social change belief structure refers to "the perception of changes as being based on the relationships between the groups as a whole; i.e. to expectations, fears or desire of such changes, to actions aiming at inducing or preventing them, or to intentions and plans to engage in these actions" (Tajfel, 1981, p. 279). A famous and frequently cited example of such a belief structure that promotes action in terms of the group rather than the individual is the Black Power movement in the United States. Other examples are some gay rights and feminist movements. According to SIT, when the social change belief structure prevails, groups will adopt one or both of the following two strategies: social creativity and social competition (Tajfel & Turner, 1986).

Social creativity and the big Other

If group boundaries are not permeable, and if there is "awareness that the existing social reality is not the only possible one and that alternatives to it are conceivable and perhaps attainable" (Tajfel, 1981, p. 283), subordinate groups can collectively search for positive distinctiveness. This includes the attempt to 'create' new representations of the group. The possibilities facing the group are, for example:

(i) To become, through action and reinterpretation of group characteristics, more like the superior group.

(ii) To reinterpret the existing inferior characteristics of the group, so that they do not appear as inferior but acquire a positively-valued distinctiveness from the superior group.

(iii) To create, through social action and/or diffusion of new 'ideologies', new group characteristics which have a positively-valued distinctiveness from the superior group.

(Tajfel, 1981, pp. 283–284)

These strategies represent "an attempt to create or preserve criteria of group definition which are not imposed from the outside" (Tajfel, 1981, p. 317). However, in order to gain a deeper understanding of social creativity strategies, we cannot exclude this 'outside' that Tajfel refers to. Even if the main goal of most social creativity strategies is for groups to define themselves in their own terms, the 'outside', which we could say is the Other, or more precisely, the perspective of the symbolic big Other, is a determining factor. Tajfel himself never actually rules out the role of some 'Otherness' in the definition of the group. He states, for example, that "'the positive aspects of social identity' and the reinterpretation of attributes and engagement in social action only acquire meaning in relation to, or in comparisons with, other groups" (Tajfel, 1981, p. 256). The re-evaluation of group characteristics, or the introduction of new and positive dimensions, does not occur in isolation from the network of relations between groups, the society and the cultural symbolic system at large (i.e. the Other). Tajfel knew that getting the redefined characteristics of the group accepted and recognized by others is a problem and a struggle:

> The battle for legitimacy ... is a battle for the acceptance by others of new forms of intergroup comparison. As long as these are not consensually accepted, the new characteristics (or the re-evaluation of the old ones) cannot be fully adequate in their function of building a new social identity.
>
> (Tajfel, 1981, p. 297)

What this account does not recognize, however, is that these 'others' do not have to be physical others 'external' to the group. The Other can be an *imagined* outgroup – rather than a 'real' other – which is perceived to have a different way of life, norms and ideals to 'us' (Verkuyten, 2005). Other groups are therefore already part of the psychological process that makes up the identity of the group. As StuartHall (1991) states, identity "as a process, as a discourse, is always told from the position of the Other" (p. 49). The group that appears to be outside us in social comparison processes is in fact essentially 'internal' to us. Identity "requires what is left outside, its constitutive outside, to consolidate the process" (Hall, 1996, p. 3). Identity construction only substantiates itself by continual negative or discriminating reference to what it is not. What this process excludes, however, will always destabilize what it includes. Identity categories are then not completely separate and unitary, but *ambivalent* and hence especially in the contemporary globalized world, the social comparison and 'differentiation' that Tajfel discusses are perhaps more complex and problematic in nature, never relying on a stable inherent term.

Social creativity strategies are thus always carried out with reference to some Other. Since "being part of a devalued group reflects the position of the group on a socio-economic scale and within a symbolic hierarchy of cultures" (Chryssochoou, 2004, p. 20), some groups, rather than others, will stand for this Other. From the perspective of the subordinated groups, the big Other could be exemplified in the group that has more power and psychological influence. The dominant social category, the group in charge of major institutions (such as governmental bodies and the media), "has the material power to promulgate its own version of the nature of society", and "it imposes the dominant value system and ideology which is carefully constructed to benefit itself, and to legitimate and perpetuate the status quo" (Hogg & Abrams, 1988, p. 27). In other words, the dominant group imposes its own ego-ideals, which function to legitimize unequal relations of power. A subordinated group's motivation to achieve positive distinctiveness (or self-esteem) shall be understood in relation to these ego-ideals of the Other, which authorize what qualifies a valued identity. Therefore, *the big Other determines what would be a positive identity*.

In some ways in the self-esteem hypothesis, SIT appears to implicitly acknowledge one of the basic facets of what makes us human: our *desire to be recognized*. We know from Lacan, however, that *desire is the desire of the Other*. A group may desire for an imaginary, narcissistic and lovable image of itself, but this image, this ideal-ego, is always judged from the perspective of the ego-ideal. In other words, a new evaluation of a group is judged from the standpoint of the desire of the Other. It is from this standpoint that the newly evaluated social category makes sense. Indeed, in agreement with SIT, there is some motivation involved in social identity processes: "identifications are always *motivated* – that is, they respond to a want-of-being" (Bracher, 1993, p. 22). In other words, identity (i.e. identification) responds to the subject's *lack* of being. The ego-ideals of the Other offer the subject a temporary sense of being: "The ego-ideal produces a sense both of permanence and self-esteem" (Bracher, 1993, p. 24). What we usually call 'self-esteem' (which is something that we may strive for, but never gain once and for all) is not at all derived from the 'self', but from the Other. Social creativity strategies are motivated by the desire to be loved and recognized by the Other. They are therefore the attempt to produce positive images *for* the Other.

To give a short example, the category 'Black' could not be renegotiated if this was not carried out in relation to the signifier 'White', and it has to be acceptable from the perspective of 'White'. The 'Black' category can only be represented favourably if done so in the terms set by the ego-ideals of an existing 'White' Other. Social creativity strategies are fundamentally *dependent* on what the desire of the big Other is imagined to be – on the ideals set in place by the compass of social and discursive values. It is the ideal of the big Other, the specific ideology of a society, which provides the frameworks for the acceptable or ideal contents/images of social groups. Not any arbitrary set of attributes, not *all* potentially available images can function as the basis of an idealizing image (ideal-ego).

We can now re-interpret Tajfel's strategies outlined above taking into account the desire of the Other. The first solution is an assimilation strategy. It involves the acceptance of the desire of the Other, a blind conformity to the Other's ideals. Taken to the extreme this would mean that the distinctiveness of the group, the group as a separate category, would eventually disappear (the next chapter illustrates with an example).

The second solution implies that existing group characteristics are given new meaning. There is no attempt here to be like the outgroup. This strategy does not represent conformity to the desire of the Other. Rather, it is an attempt to make the distinctive qualities of the group equal in value to other groups, it is to reinterpret the 'inferior' qualities of the group and get them accepted within the symbolic structure of a given society. It is important to note here that this is *not* a rejection of the desire of the Other. On the contrary, the desire of the Other is considered to be fundamental as the strategy involves an attempt to *change* it. Rather than changing the qualities of the category, this strategy represents an aspiration to alter the ego-ideals of the symbolic Other so that the characteristics of the subordinated group no longer appear as inferior from the perspective of the Other (the next chapter illustrates with an example).

The third solution – which can be very similar to the second – implies the creation of new, more valued, characteristics. Groups often search for these 'new' qualities in their past history. For example, people from stigmatized Muslim communities in Europe often take delight in telling the story of past Islamic empires. Depending on the 'content' (the images or signifiers used), this strategy could involve either an attempt to change the ego-ideals of the Other, or a conformity to these ego-ideals. It depends on the exact features of these 'new' characteristics; whether or not they fit within the scope of the desire of the Other. It could in some cases include an effort to alter the desire of the Other so that the 'new' characteristics are 'valued' by the Other. Tajfel uses the example of a study (Lemaine and Kastersztein, 1972–1973, cited in Tajfel, 1981, p. 286) that consisted of a competition between two groups of boys to build huts. One of the groups was given fewer building materials than the other. The 'inferior' group (the one with fewer resources) built an inferior hut but surrounded it with a small garden. Tajfel (1981) states that this group then "engaged in sharp discussions with the children from the other group and the adult judges to obtain acknowledgement of the legiti-macy of their work" (p. 286). From our perspective, these children were trying to change the ego-ideals of the Other, so that the new characteristics fit within the range of what is seen as an 'ideal' hut. This includes of course a desire to make these new characteristics *recognized* by the Other.

The new characteristics could nevertheless also match the ego-ideals of the Other; they could conform to the desire of the dominant group. As Tajfel

(1981) states, the new characteristics "may consist of attributes which are already consensually highly valued by both (or more) groups, and which the inferior group was previously deemed not to possess" (p. 285). Žižek (2008) gives an example that is useful here. He suggests that the Dalai Lama attempts to make Buddhism comprehensible in the West, and thus promotes the characteristics of the religion in ways that fit within the Western worldview. The Dalai Lama "justifies Tibetan Buddhism in Western terms of the pursuit of happiness and the avoidance of pain" (Žižek, 2008, p. 73). In other words, the Dalai Lama represents Buddhism in new ways that conforms to the desire of the Other.

Apart from those suggested by Tajfel, Turner and Brown (1978) also mention the strategy of "changing the *outgroup* with which the ingroup is compared, in particular ceasing to use the dominant group as relevant comparison group" (p. 205). The act of comparing oneself involves the use of an ideal. In comparing itself with another, possibly more inferior category, the group does so with reference to certain ideals that define a 'valued' identity. Subordinated groups compare themselves with each other, using certain characteristics as the standard. Even in this strategy, therefore, the role played by the Other in determining the criteria used for comparison cannot be ruled out. For example, instead of comparing with the wealthy white middle class category, a white member of the poor working class group may choose to compare him or herself with the 'Pakistani' social category. Certain qualities, such as 'smell', will be used as criteria for comparison. 'We don't own fancy cars and clothes, but at least we don't smell like those Paki people', this person may say. In order for this person to be able to use it as a criterion for comparison and evaluation, some Other has already authorized 'smell' as significant for self-definition. This implies that in our example, the Pakistani category is not really an Other at all. It is merely used as an image to conjure up a satisfactory ideal-ego image of the 'poor white' category. The Pakistani category is an imaginary other, which, in Lacanian theory, is not really an Other, since in imaginary identification subjects misrecognize themselves in the ideal-egos of others, or on the contrary, they do not accept the non-ideal or threatening elements of the other in themselves. The symbolic big Other in this example is the position that authorizes 'smell' as important in the representation of identity.

Let us note that 'smell' is a signifier, an element of the symbolic. *Social creativity processes are discursive processes*: they cannot be carried out without the use of signifiers and images in discourse. In some social creativity strategies, the attempt is to make previously denigrated group characteristics, such as black skin, the *keffiyeh*, or other cultural practices, emblems and images of minority/subordinated groups, "value-laden" (Tajfel, 1981, p. 277). The process includes assigning value to certain characteristics, which will become loaded signifiers. Chapter 4 discussed how a 'signifier' is something which gains significance, and which becomes the target of emotional investment. This implies that a characteristic of a group, such as the *keffiyeh*, will function as an object of libido, which means that people will affectively invest in these objects. Affect, or *jouissance*, is what is at stake in strategies that entail changing the desire of the Other – in changing the symbolic. These strategies often result in social conflict when they involve a threat to the existing social and political structures, and a threat to the *jouissance* of certain groups.

Taking the desire of the Other into account implies that even when minorities seemingly attempt to define themselves *in their own terms* – whether this involves introducing new, more acceptable, dimensions or re-evaluating existing ones – it is carried out *in relation* to the cultural standards of what is considered a positive, desirable, or socially valorized identity. When a minority attempts to transform previously negative aspects of identity into positive ones, even when they aim to define these aspects according to their own criteria – this does not usually occur in isolation from general, and accepted, cultural norms and values, or from the 'majority' point of view.

This is also the case for groups that actively separate themselves from the rest of society, such as certain Muslim groups in Britain who live in self-segregated communities. These groups define their identities *in relation* to the 'secular Western' Other. Although on the surface this may seem to establish a distinguished and completely separate category, the 'secular Western' is a repressed unconscious signifier that defines the very identities of these Muslim groups. We have already discussed the notion of alienation in Chapter 3. In the example here, the existence of the Muslim identity is premised on the repression of the 'secular Western' category which is externalized (i.e. Otherized). In Lacanian theory "repression entails, in general, this externalization of that which is repressed, as well as the division of the subject between his two contradictory parts, namely, his conscious identity and his unconscious alienation in that which has been externalized" (Pavón Cuéllar, 2010, p. 141). A subordinated group's alienation in the gaze of the Other is most clearly demonstrated in Clark and Clark's (1939) famous psychology study on black children's preference for white dolls and white skin, which suggests that children from subordinated communities identify with the ideals of the dominant group. They internalize, and accept the 'external' depiction of their group as 'inferior'.

What our discussion implies is that many of the strategies adopted by stigmatized, and subordinated groups are in fact not exactly equal to attempts to reject inferiority, because these groups have already internalized the ideals and gaze of the Other. Žižek (2008) discusses Muslim 'fundamentalism' and argues that "the problem is not cultural difference (their effort to preserve their identity), but the opposite fact that the fundamentalists are already like us, that, secretly, they have already internalized our standards and measure themselves by them" (p. 73). When the Other gets psychologically and physically too close, when it has already imposed its values on me, I will negate this imposition and deny its power over me, by affirming my distinctiveness. This way, I can prove to myself and to the rest of the world my independence from the Other. Turner and Brown (1978) mention how the racial segregation in the United States was a response by the whites to the loss of social distance between whites and blacks in the post-bellum period. In other words, physical segregation was a response to the threatening psychological presence of the Other. The more powerful the social and psychological presence of the Other, the greater is the need to create spatial and physical distance and differentiation.

Socio-symbolic symptom

The arguments put forward in this chapter imply that actions which appear to reject a subordinated identity can in fact have multiple, and often contradictory aims. Indeed, the SIT paradigm completely overlooks the fact that it is perfectly possible to *consciously reject something, but unconsciously accept the very same thing.* A clinical psychoanalytic situation, and the idea of *symptom* can be used as examples to further elaborate on the ambivalence of political resistance struggles, or social change efforts. We can use the analogy of someone commencing psychoanalysis. Let us assume that before starting, this person is sometimes in great emotional and mental pain. The *perception* is that change is possible, and the decision to start analysis is a way of *rejecting* the damaging influence of the pain on this person's life. It could even be viewed as a 'self-conscious' decision to start fighting a destructive psychological state.

In psychoanalysis, the notion of the symptom is very complicated and can have multiple definitions. It can, for example, be understood as the return of memories or thoughts that we prefer to forget, the reappearance of unwanted and uncomfortable thoughts that can lead to painful physical states and destructive behaviours. Lacan's understanding of symptoms is that they are kinds of knots of *jouissance*: symptoms tie up enjoyment and suffering together. The ambiguous pleasure–pain of psychical symptoms remains gratifying even while they are disruptive: we tend to enjoy our symptoms – as Freud (1957) insists, people never willingly abandon a source of libidinal satisfaction. Thus, the person in our example will tenaciously resist giving up such symptoms. The Lacanian idea of *repetition* is the tendency of the subject to compulsively repeat certain ideas, or signifiers. More accurately, it is the 'insistence' of signifiers to repeat themselves. The signifier itself is the dominant category for Lacan, not the agency of the 'self'. *Jouissance* is the real reason for the inertia of signifiers, our resistance to changing them. The idea that the subject may enjoy its symptom may seem very counter-intuitive, especially from the perspective of SIT. Psychoanalysis teaches us, however, that "subjects sometimes enjoy *unconsciously* what they *consciously* experience as *displeasure*" (Glynos, 2001, p. 7). The notion of the 'flight into health', the idea that the 'patient' would rather make one or two minor changes to their life than give up their underlying libidinal patterns of gratification, is crucial here. Thus, once the person in our example starts analysis, he or she does "not *use* knowledge to effect a freedom from suffering; the subject in fact *denies* knowledge in order to continue to suffer" (Alcorn, 1994, p. 34). A symptom is then that which persists: it "is that which we would like to get rid of, but which sheer will-power does not budge" (Glynos, 2003, p. 7). The symptom disrupts the unity and sense of coherence of the subject; it keeps the subject and fixes it in a certain place and it leads to repetitive regression back to a previous state of being. The symptom is that part of the subject which resists change and treats any attempts at transformation as unwelcome because the subject, in some sense, unconsciously enjoys the symptom, even if it is consciously painful. In clinical psychoanalysis, although the aim is to induce change, it is recognized that given patterns of gratification, of libidinal enjoyment, there is a resistance to change; the entrenched libidinal patterns, modes of *jouissance* are particularly resistant to transformation. All this indicates the ambiguous nature of our intentions: "a person wants something (for example, to change) but [they do] not want it at the same time" (Frosh, 2003, p. 84).

Political resistance can sometimes take the form of a symptom. Indeed, the psychoanalytic notion of resistance could be useful to elaborate on political resistance. Although it is a very complicated (and contentious) idea, resistance in psychoanalysis could be simplified for our purposes and defined as *resistance to change in oneself or in the way in which one gains enjoyment*. It is the blockage that hinders progress in treatment. Analytic resistance is something negative as it inhibits change. Rose (1996) argues that psychoanalytic resistance is more related to "defensiveness" than to liberation; "you resist when you don't want to budge" (p. 5). Political and psychoanalytic resistance can merge and occur at one and the same time. The process of rejecting a given social order or identity can *contain* resistance to change. Thus, (psychic) resistance can exist within (political) resistance. In short,

> from a psychoanalytic point of view, socio-political symptoms persist exactly because they provide the social subject with a form of enjoyment. This explains why it is so hard to dis-articulate or displace such symptoms.
> (Glynos & Stavrakakis, 2003, p. 120)

It should be stressed though that the symptom is also "a sign of the uncon-scious", an indication that *"the unconscious is here and it has something to say"* (Dean, 2002, p. 27). In clinical psychoanalysis, a symptom is a sign of a 'hidden' conflict. We can state that a socio-symbolic symptom both hides and reminds us of a particular type of conflict between various groups; conflicts not too different to the kinds SIT is concerned with.

Thus, what the SIT paradigm may call a 'social change' strategy could be better understood as a socio-symbolic symptom. SIT's image of the subject as rational, coherent and unitary prevents it from considering how the boundary between acceptance and rejection of a subordinated identity or unjust social system is often very blurred. The ambivalence of rejection is an effect of subordinated groups' very identity being a result of the socio-symbolic system. For example, in a racist society, the ideology that blacks are inferior will affect black people "in the very core of their beings", and therefore it would be simplistic to assume that "they can (and do) resist [this inferiority] as free autonomous agents through their acts, dreams and projects" (Žižek, 2008, p. 62).

We implied above that the self-segregation, or fundamentalism, of some Muslim groups cannot simply be understood as a rejection of their 'inferior' identity, because their actions bear testimony to the fact that the explicit or implicit image of the 'inferior Muslim' circulated in the West and elsewhere has, at some level, already been accepted by these groups. Tajfel (1981) in some ways recognizes the blurred boundary between acceptance and rejec-tion of a subordinated identity. He states that one response to such an identity is the "withdrawal from the wider community system of norms, values, prescriptions, achievements, and the creation of groups which have their own values, divergent from those which are generally approved" (Tajfel, 1981, p. 326). Minorities in this situation could stop comparing themselves with the majority. Although this may appear as a way to *reject* an inferior identity and an attempt to regain self-respect, Tajfel argues that it can lead to a *reinforcement* of the negative image and position of the group. Tajfel is here alluding to the unintended consequences of an action or communicative act. One may intend to reject an image of oneself, but can end up affirming this image. This is because "when we act, we never do so with full knowledge of the consequences, of our motives, or of how others understand the situation. Rather we simply act" (Dean, 2006, p. 21). In this sense, *the notion of 'cognitive alternatives' is misleading.* Those who resist a given social order, or a specific representation of identity, very *rarely* have in mind clear alternatives. It is not exactly knowledge of, for example, alternative social systems or identities that inspire them to act. Given that some revolu-tions in the past have led to surprising consequences, one can ask what kind of 'self-consciousness' or 'knowledge' they were motivated by (the 1979

Islamic Revolution in Iran, which led to the establishment of a fundamentalist, oppressive Islamic Republic is an example). The 'cognitive alternative' idea in the SIT approach has already been put into question by Reicher (1996, p. 325). But if it is not 'cognitive alternatives', what else may drive some collective actions?

The hidden motives of social competition acts

Riots, along with terrorism, revolutions and war, would be classified in SIT as forms of 'social competition'. Social competition, the "direct competition with the outgroup" (Turner & Brown, 1978, p. 205) represents a struggle for 'objective' social change. It should be clear before we move on that these strategies cannot be clearly distinguished from social creativity. Social competition and social creativity are more likely to occur simultaneously. For example, the social creativity strategy of turning 'black skin' into something positive would, at least in theory, have 'objective' or material social implications: a group that is no longer seen in negative terms is also more likely to gain access to jobs and other material privileges they were previously excluded from.

Instead of being motivated by a clear social change objective or by 'cognitive alternatives', social competition acts can lack a clear purpose of change, and have another aim: that of attracting the attention of the Other. For example, Žižek in his discussion of the 2005 riots in the suburbs of Paris argues that

> what is most difficult to accept is precisely the riots' meaninglessness: more than a form of protest, they are what Lacan called a *passage à l'acte* – an impulsive movement into action which can't be translated into speech or thought and carries within an intolerable weight of frustration.
>
> (Žižek 2008, p. 65)

There is no doubt that the riots occurred against a backdrop of social exclusion, racial discrimination and lack of recognition of France's poorest communities. The actions of the youths were an expression of dissatisfaction towards this state of affairs, and could be interpreted as conveying a wish for social change. But the violence *itself* was less about social change than "an effort to gain visibility" (Žižek, 2008, p. 65). An excluded and neglected social group drew attention to its existence. When language is inadequate for this type of task, there is often recourse to violence. "Their actions spoke for them: like it or not, we're here, no matter how much you pretend not to see us," (p. 65). The 2011 UK riots by youths from mostly poor black communities led to damage on a massive scale. This damage succeeded, however, in directing the world's gaze on this group of neglected youths; it managed to remind the Other of their existence. Of course, the attention these youths obtained was mainly condemnation and disapproval, but it was attention nevertheless. Rather than leading to any progressive form of change, their actions are more likely to lead to increased prejudice, the reinforcement of images of inferiority, and further suppression of this group.

The question SIT researchers are not interested in is why social competition acts are often 'irrational' and annihilative. Why are they often destructive rather than 'creative', for example? This is a crucial question since if these acts are motivated by a wish for social change, then it is curious that they often involve damage and destruction. After all, 'social change' implies an alteration, and in some ways, creation and construction. The lack of a proper theory of affect, or passion, in the SIT paradigm, means that it cannot tell us why social competition strategies often occur with such zeal and intensity. In psychoanalysis there is something known as the 'death drive'. This is not necessarily related to our drive for death, but rather, it is the human drive to go beyond the pleasure principle, and enter the field of excessive *jouis-sance*. The death drive is the human tendency for destruction and suffering. "Various kinds of martyrdom, suicide bombings and even orgiastic hooli-ganism [are] examples which might be said to bear witness to a fundamental death drive" (Daly, 1999, p. 234). What these examples demonstrate is that although social competition acts may, admittedly, at some level seem to reflect a wish for social change, at another level, they may be driven by the excessive enjoyment of the death drive.

Our discussion points to a crucial aspect overlooked by the SIT paradigm, namely the orthodox nature of many subordinated groups' so-called social change and social competition strategies. To Turner and Brown (1978) "the development of ethnocentrism in subordinate groups ... may constitute an important force for social change" (p. 202). SIT does not take seriously how this development can represent a reactionary, rather than progressive approach to change. From our Lacanian perspective, the collapse of a belief structure or a symbolic system creates uncertainty and anxiety. Therefore the elimination of one symbolic system often occurs alongside the creation of another one. The latter can become the source of new forms of certainties and deep emotional investments that 'stick' and that are not easily demolished. "Something new can also stick – especially within conditions of social and political dislocation of older identities ... [and] obviously the new does not always imply progressive transformation" (Stavrakakis, 2007, p. 168). An example is some Black Power movements that advocate separ-atism, nationalism and violence. Another example is Zionism. Billig (2002) states that "Zionism had been engaged in the very activity described by

Social Identity Theory; it was explicitly overturning centuries of stereotyping, which had depicted Jews as passive, unheroic, politically uncreative and so on", but he believes that there is "a political untruth in applying a theory of liberation to the most reactionary political movement imaginable" (p. 180). We must note that movements such as Zionism and Black Power do not actually represent a total collapse of the symbolic. They are based on the very symbolic system that created them. For example, the Black Power movement is *founded* on racial difference. Rather than challenging the symbolic structure of racialization, it wants to emphasize it. These movements are a product of a symbolic and historical context: they are a *reaction* to this context. They are, we could say, a socio-symbolic symptom.

Conclusion

The main point of this chapter has been to show how the actions that SIT researchers may call social change strategies may be better understood as socio-symbolic symptoms. In other words, rather than representing change, or a wish for change, these actions can be a product of a certain kind of relation or conflict between powerful and powerless groups. Let us stress though that not all of the subordinated groups' actions may be interpreted in terms of a symptom. Each case of social change or intergroup relation *must* be analysed independently. The aim in this chapter has therefore not been to advocate some sort of a grand theory, but to point out some of the problems and inadequacies of the SIT paradigm, for example its disregard for the fact that *some* actions by subordinated groups are better understood as socio-symbolic symptoms than as a transparent wish for change. It becomes possible to fully grasp the latter point once social stability and social change are no longer viewed as a matter of cognition and perception, but of desire, fantasy, and perhaps most importantly, *jouissance*. When the 'cognitive model' is abandoned, it becomes possible to notice the 'absurd' aspect of social change strategies: how subordinated groups may play a part in reproducing their own subordination. As Stavrakakis states

> taking into account the enjoyment promised or (partially) experienced ... can decisively help to explain our sticking (even with some ironic distance) to symbolic constructions (ideals, rationalisations and the like), which are obviously disabling and enslaving.
>
> (Stavrakakis, 2007, p. 181)

The powerful impact of *jouissance* should by now be clear. This bodily factor runs counter to the cognitivism of SIT and the discursivism of discursive psychology. *Jouissance* can explain the absence of collective action in situations where there exists a perception of change. A libidinal attachment to the 'deviant' group, for example, can help to reproduce this group's enslavement by the system. From a psychoanalytic position, *jouissance* is the "payment the exploited, the servant, receives for serving the Master" (Žižek, 1997, p. 48). In other words, subordinated groups are not only victims of exploitation and subordination; *they are also the victims of their own jouissance.*

7 *Gringo*: a case study

This chapter uses the case of a Swedish anti-racist magazine, *Gringo*, to elaborate on some of the theoretical points made in previous chapters. Let us stress that the content of *Gringo* discussed here functions *merely* as illustration: the aim is to make a number of claims about SIT, and suggest some ways Lacanian theory could be used to analyse processes of identification, social creativity and social change in media discourse. Readers more interested in *Gringo* magazine, the multicultural and media context of Sweden, or the methodological and analytical procedures employed in the analysis of the material, should consult Dashtipour (2009).

A short background

Zanyar Adami, a young journalist who had immigrated to Sweden as a child, founded *Gringo* magazine in 2004 as a form of social entrepreneurship/ integration project. It was published until 2007 as a monthly supplement in the Swedish free daily *Metro*, and sold four times a year as the collection *Gringo Grande*. The magazine emerged against a political and cultural background where there had been an increased demand for the recognition of the 'immigrant' identity, a social category explicitly or implicitly viewed as inferior and 'other' to the 'native' Swedish category. One of the ways in which the 'immigrant' has been made inferior is through the pejorative terms *svartskalle* (black-skull or black-head) and *blatte* (the meaning of this term is not established). These words, which can be used interchangeably, have negative connotations and refer to minorities with immigration backgrounds from the Middle East, Africa, Latin America or Eastern Europe. In the recent decade, *blatte* and *svartskalle* have, however, been employed by some sort of a political movement (see Mulinari & Neergaard, 2005, p. 71). *Gringo* followed the trend – already in progress in the cultural sphere – aiming to 'redeem' these terms. Adami states "when I call myself *svartskalle*, I immediately take back the word"[4] (*Gringo* 18).[5] This involves the objective of turning the negatively evaluated categories into a positive basis for social identity.

Another related objective of *Gringo* was to challenge the mainstream media's negative image of *förorten*, the suburbs. These suburbs refer to the areas in Sweden's major cities that are the result of the so-called *miljonpro-grammet* (The Million Programme), a housing project implemented by the government in the 1960s and 1970s. The media more often than not depicts these areas, today mostly inhabited by immigrants, as Sweden's 'ghettos', and thereby sustains a cemented image of the suburb as that which symbolizes the 'other' of Swedishness (Dahlstedt, 2004). One profound indication of the 'difference' of youth from these communities is their way of speaking Swedish. *Blatte-Svenska* (*Blatte-Swedish*) usually refers to a hybrid, colloquial language characterized by slang and words borrowed from other languages. It is an indicator of ethnic and class belong-ing. *Blatte-Swedish*, also called *Rinkeby-Swedish* and *Rosengård-Swedish*,[6] is seen as a confirmation of the youth being deviant from the 'norm' and serves to confirm their marginal position in society (Ålund & Schierup, 1991). *Blatte-Swedish* is thus devalued; it is perceived as inauthentic, not a proper way of speaking. It works, for example, to limit career opportunities because speakers are believed to lack appropriate communication skills (Milani, 2010). The delegitimization of *blatte-Swedish* functions thus to define the boundaries of Swedish linguistic and cultural norms, and classify those who are and are not worthy of integration into the Swedish community. *Blatte-Swedish*, indicating membership in the *blatte* social category, is nevertheless used quite intentionally by youth from the suburbs to contest authority and the normative and exclusionary operations of power. For the youth, *blatte* and *blatte-Swedish* are applied as consciousness raising tools, they are symbols of resistance against Swedish cultural ideals (Lacatus, 2007). *Gringo's* highly controversial use of *blatte-Swedish* was a strategy to simultaneously represent the '*Gringo* brand', express the specific *Gringo* identity, and resist the ideals of Swedish linguistic norms. *Gringo*, with its 'bottom-up', humorous and playful journalism, was to signify the revolution against ethnic discrimination and exclusion, and it was to offer a 'new', and more heterogeneous version of Swedishness. However, in August 2007 the magazine began to reduce the number of issues published. Not long after, publication stopped completely because its publishing company went into bankruptcy. The reason is not entirely clear, but some claim it was due to a decline in sales (Schori, 2008). *Gringo* was subsequently relaunched outside *Metro* as a free magazine with a new chief editor. The new chief editor resigned in June 2009 and the future of *Gringo* is as yet unclear. This chapter focuses on the first version of the magazine as published in *Metro*.

Following SIT, we can view the advent of *Gringo* as evidence of the existence of 'cognitive alternatives'. *Gringo* perceived exclusion, discrimination and stigmatization of those with immigration backgrounds as illegitimate. The magazine's aim to challenge stereotypes and prejudice, and its attempt to make visible and condemn institutional discrimination and exclusion based on ethnicity, bear testimony to the existence of a perception that the social relations between those categorized as 'Swede' and those categorized as 'immigrant' can change. In its attempt to reject the negative evaluation of the immigrant identity, *Gringo* made use of various social creativity strategies.

Becoming like the Swede

Gringo adopts a strategy that could be classified as both strategy (i) and (ii) discussed in Chapter 6. To be precise, *Gringo* introduces new dimensions (iii) in order to make the 'immigrant' category like the 'superior' Swedish category (i). Two examples from the magazine are used here to demonstrate how this process is crucially a matter of desire: the desire of the Swedish Other.

A section in *Gringo* named *Svenskar med annan bakrund än typisk svensk … typ* (Swedes with a different background than typically Swedish) includes articles on people with an immigration background, or another background unlike the 'typical' ethnic Swedish. In other words, a social category usually considered to be 'different'/'other' to the Swedish category is represented here. The following example is the story of a couple of young Chinese-Swedes.[7]

Bo & Peng

"Chuan qiu", yells Bo Huang and grabs the ball …

"Most people think that Chinese people are short, but just look at us", Bo says and points at his brother Lei Huang and their friend Peng Zhou. Every Saturday a dozen young Chinese-Swedes meet in the Tibble court to play basketball … No one is shorter than 1.80 cm.

Chinese-Swedes are one of the most anonymous minorities in Sweden. You only get to meet them at Chinese restaurants. "Most Chinese-Swedes socialize only with each other. Most know each other because we are not that many. The language is a barrier, Chinese is very different to Swedish, which makes it difficult for a Chinese person to understand Swedish", says Bo Huang and he dries the sweat from his forehead.

... "If we add an 'f' to Lei, we would be called Bo and Leif.[8] More Swedish names are difficult to find", says Bo. He remembers his first impression of Sweden very well. "I came here in January and remember the snow and the air was so clean. People said 'hej' to me and dad and I couldn't understand why they were so rude to us. In China 'hej' means something like 'hey' and it's very rude", says Bo and he laughs widely while his eyes turn into thin openings.

What prejudices exist against Chinese people? "We look like this", Peng Zhou says and laughs at the same time as he makes a facelift with his hands, making his eyes even smaller. "Just because we are Chinese, people assume we are good at kung fu and can play table tennis, I can't do any of that", says Bo Huang. "I know kung fu", says Peng Zhou who has recently started to practice.

... Bo Huang thinks well of Sweden and he sees his future here. He wants to stay here, build a family and create a life ...

No one knows exactly how many Chinese people there are in China. The government recently employed six million Chinese people and gave them the task to count the other Chinese people in two weeks. They got an approximate number: 1,298,847,624 ...

(Gringo 1)

In this article, and in other similar ones, the people are portrayed in a relaxed, friendly, informal setting, aiming to represent immigrants as 'any other ordinary people'. These types of articles implicitly refer to and challenge other texts in media depicting immigrants as 'other'. The function here is to strip the immigrants of their 'difference'. The images accompanying these texts confirm this. They usually depict people as happy, in an everyday kind of context (such as in a basketball court, bowling hall or a park). The objective is to represent, make recognized, a social group which has been negatively represented or is usually not visible in the public sphere. For example, the demographic information at the end of the article seems to do just that. This text also negates the usual stereotypes of Chinese people, such as the stereotype of 'Chinese people are short'. The repetitive refutation of stereotypes works not only to contest them, but it is also part of the attempt to produce an 'ordinary', 'normal' image of the immigrant category. The boys in this article are depicted as 'down-to-earth' and they make fun and laugh at prejudices against the Chinese. The attempt to remove the 'difference' of Chinese people includes reducing the gap between the Chinese and the Swede: Bo is quoted as saying that their names are like Swedish names.

The implicit meaning seems to be 'Chinese are just like Swedes, even their names are similar'. One could say, following SIT, that, for example, being tall, having similar names as Swedes, are *new* group criteria introduced to depict an image of the Chinese that is identical to, or comes close to, that of the Swede. This method is, as we know, not very different from an attempt to *assimilate* the Chinese identity into what is considered to be the majority norm, because making the Chinese 'ordinary', not 'different' is the same as making them 'blend in', absorbing them in the majority group.

Let us stress, however, that this is a very ambiguous strategy, because despite the attempt to make the Chinese 'normal', or 'similar' to the Swede, assumptions of difference strongly permeate this text. The reference to the above differences which may ostensibly be minor (their language, their eyes, their overpopulated country) immediately become tantamount to essential differences which matter and which link to longstanding stereotypes. The reaffirmation of stereotypes, despite the attempt to resist them, is typical of these kinds of articles in *Gringo*. This issue is further discussed later in this chapter.

The following article is another example of the attempt to make the 'immigrant' like the 'superior' group, but here it is not enough to simply be 'ordinary'. A number of articles in *Gringo* depict immigrants as exceptional people, rebels or agents of social change. We can call these 'hero' articles. These include reports on young music bands, singers, actors, sportsmen or women. In the following, Nessim, a middle-aged man, is portrayed as an outstanding representative for the Swedish community.

Nessim

Love for and loyalty to Sweden is what drives Nessim Becket to find 500 jobs every year for jobseekers all by himself.

… During his time here Nessim has helped find jobs for about 500 people every year … There are no replacements so when he is ill or during the holidays, the 'café' is closed. He says: "It can of course be difficult to work alone with a lack of resources. I am quite stingy but never with my strength. The driving force behind my work is my loyalty to Sweden. I feel great love for this country and think that more people would feel like that if they had a job."

On the walls there are thank you cards and flowers from visitors ….

"I don't have much space for myself right now. My working day starts already in the underground because I meet several of the unemployed there. The job then continues at the office, in the centre of town and on the way home. I don't even have time for my family, but actually everybody is my family ... There is often an underlying reason for why a person hasn't been able to find a job. I try to find out what that is and work from there. I don't want anybody to ever leave empty handed" ... Nobody is judged here: "Instead of saying 'why did you do that' or 'contact the social welfare secretary' I choose to say 'let's see what we can do'. I never see people as a problem".

(Gringo 3)

This is a typical article in *Gringo* depicting the 'immigrant' as beyond 'ordinary'. The immigrant is ambitious and successful. Nessim is portrayed as a 'hero'. He is given an important role: a representative of the socio-cultural institution of the Swedish community. Nessim is a hardworking and benevolent man whose main purpose in life is to help people. This is in stark contrast to media representations and other stereotypes, which link immigrant men with laziness, crime, patriarchal women abusers or exploiters of government funding. Therefore, apart from being a strategy that introduces new dimensions to make the immigrant more like the Swede (or perhaps even better than the Swede), it could also be classified as what Hall (1997) calls *reversal* of stereotypes. A number of 'hero' articles in *Gringo* all have similar content to this one (success, ambition, immigrants as agents of change) and similar functions (reversal of stereotypes). Just like the 'ordinary' strategy, by introducing new dimensions (in the example about Nessim these dimensions would, for example, be success, ambition, compassion for people), the stereotypes usually attached to 'immigrant' men in Sweden (laziness, dishonesty, exploiters of government funding) are reversed. Now, the content of these images are crucial in themselves, but a Lacanian reading would focus on the following question: *for whom are these images depicted*? Both an SIT and a discourse analytical reading would point out what these images *do*, their function (for example, challenging stereotypes, introducing new characteristics). None of these approaches would, however, centre on the fact that images are always images *for* someone. Thus, although a Lacanian perspective also concentrates on the *functions* of discourse, it would pay attention to the way discourse functions to say something to the Other.

The 'ordinary' image and especially the 'hero' image depict *imaginary* images – they are narcissistic ideal-egos of the 'immigrant' identity. The immigrant is covertly (and sometimes overtly) compared to the 'Swede' and shown to be as 'ordinary', 'competent' and 'morally good'. If we take what we highlighted in the previous chapter, that *it is the big Other which determines what would be a 'positive' identity*, we can see how these images conform to the desire of the Other, how they are *for* the Other. The foreign immigrant can thus only be represented favourably if done so in the terms set by the ego-ideals of an existing Swedish Other. What makes the two positive images above work as a source of ideal-ego identifications is that they are located with reference to the symbolic ego-ideal benchmarks of what are accepted and demanded social ideals in society. As such they come into play only via the Other, that is to say, when the entrenched perspective, the standard ideological position of the community in question, is dominantly present.

Therefore, in the case of *Gringo*, becoming like the 'superior' group means identifying *with the ideals of the Swedish outgroup*. Immigrants are made lovable, they become the narcissistic means, the ideal-ego resources whereby Swedes see what they like about themselves in someone else. This means that in this fundamentally narcissistic process – the immigrant is never seen beyond their usefulness as an idealizing mirror – it is only via the Swedish ego-ideals, the values of Swedish culture, that the immigrant takes on any real value. In the 'ordinary' and the 'hero' discourse, it appears thus that there is no way to represent the cultural positives of these subjects in their own terms, the only way they can appear likeable is by being subject to, filtered through the ideals of this Other, otherwise they do not attain any positive representability.

Of course, the desire of the Other is not explicitly stated in the text. It is a hidden element of the text. This does not mean that it is not there. It exists, so to speak, 'between the lines'. It is embodied in the ego-ideal signifiers of the text, and we can detect these signifiers. For example, in order to be desired by the Other, one needs to enjoy life in Sweden and love and be loyal to this country. A positively evaluated immigrant is one who is faithful to Sweden. Further, in the first article, being 'ordinary' is depicted as desirable (for example, the young men do not particularly stand out, they do not complain about injustices, and they are happy and enjoying life). In the second article, 'ordinary' is not enough and being helpful, hard working and 'morally good', and perhaps socially aware, are prescribed as desirable modes of being in the eyes of the Other. In most of the articles about 'the immigrant', the people all have some kind of job, are studying to obtain a decent or highly regarded education, or are busy with some or other commendable, socially acceptable activity. There is an absence of images of people who are unemployed or 'socially failed' in other ways.

To wrap up this section we can make two points. First, in order to be seen, one has to be represented via the mediating lens of the ego-ideals of the Swedish big Other. Thus – unless one is to be relegated to a negative identity, of those negatively defined by their opposition to, or failure as regards these values – there is a need to meet and affirm these minimal standards if one is to attain any form of positive visibility, to be seen as normal. Second, the Other, the point from which 'normal' is judged, entrenches a highly specific set of cultural and societal values. This Other, at least in popular media discourse, is on the one hand imagined to desire 'ordinariness' and 'not standing out'. On the other hand (and paradoxically) the Other desires excellence and prominence, the exceptionality of the status of the hero, the helper. As an immigrant one needs to do something in addition to merely being able to claim acknowledgement, one must do something extra to attain citizenship recognition, be involved in some kind of civic duty. This is what leads to an odd logic at work. *One has to be exceptional to be normal.* The immigrant can only be accepted as 'normal' if he is more than just 'average', if he is an outstanding human being.

This makes apparent a challenge for *Gringo*: the problem of representing the immigrant, creating a 'positive' identity of this social group, without identification with the ego-ideal values of the host culture, the dominant outgroup: without *conforming* to the desire of the big Other. In fact, *Gringo does* resist the desire of the Other in its campaign for the recognition of *blatte*. This will be discussed later in the chapter. In what follows, *Gringo*'s ambivalence regarding the image of the immigrant is explored further.

Insistence on difference

As mentioned above, in its depiction of the immigrant, *Gringo* has a strong tendency to repeat assumptions of difference, despite its attempt to reject them. Consider the following extracts from an article about a couple of Thai women:

They are called whores

… Thirty year old Nicklas Norberg is living with a Thai-Swedish woman. One evening when he is out with his partner a guy approaches them. "She is the one who cleans and cooks at home, isn't she?" the guy asks.

…. People think that Nicklas has bought her, that she is a prostitute whose main task is to clean and take care of the house.

… We are sitting in a Thai restaurant. The decor gives the feeling of Thailand …. Tik, who has lived here for almost two years, thinks that Swedish food is good, but not as good as Thai food. And she is enjoying it here; even if the disadvantages are many, the advantages are greater. "Life is difficult in Thailand. I earned 3,000 Kronas a month as a host and master of ceremonies. Here, I earn 14,000 Kronas", says Tik.

.... Before she found Nicklas, Jeab earned 20 Kronas on average per day, six days a week in various jobs, including waitressing and work at a factory. "Life in the factory was hard. Everything became so much better when Nicklas turned up", says Jeab. Not with a melancholic voice, but she is really shining when she mentions Nicklas and then she laughs. Both Jeab and Tik laugh a lot during the conversation.

... Next year in March, Jeab and Nicklas are going down to Thailand to get married. Nicklas is going with fourteen of his closest friends who will meet the other 350 guests.

(Gringo 4)

Like the previous articles, this is attempting to challenge assumptions of difference and thereby making the immigrant 'ordinary', more like the Swede. Just like our earlier examples, the context is a relaxed and informal one (a Thai restaurant), the people are depicted as happy (the Thai women "laugh a lot"). Enjoying life in Sweden is another theme we have already come across. However, this text demonstrates clearly how the task of making the immigrant similar to the Swede is an ambiguous one.

As already mentioned in the discussion about the Chinese boys, in a great number of articles that report on those with immigration backgrounds, the denial of difference and reproduction/confirmation of difference occur simultaneously. For example, in the above text, it is claimed that these women face the (presumably exaggerated) stereotype of Thai women as "prostitutes", who only want to marry someone in order to be able to leave Thailand. Although the attempt is to contest this stereotype, the picture drawn is one that presents life in Thailand as "difficult" and coming to Sweden makes life much "easier". It becomes difficult to break free from stereotypes of 'inferiority' when the Thai woman is described as being saved from the "hard life" of Thailand when meeting Nicklas who made everything "so much better". In addition, the attention paid to the link between Thai women and being seen as "whores" (especially in the heading) in some ways confirms this very same link, because one could argue that a story of Thai women could be told without making such strong reference to the 'whore stereotype'. There seems to be a paradox therefore between on the one hand intending to criticize stereotypes of Thai women and depict them as ordinary, happy, honourable, righteous and 'normal' – thus, making them desirable to the big Other (the position from which an ideal woman is seen) – and on the other hand, 'unintentionally' reproducing ideas of 'difference'.

Such an outcome seems, however, to be unavoidable. One can argue that what *Gringo* is attempting is understandable. Nevertheless, in simulta-neously normalizing and yet also admitting difference, a kind of deadlock is reached whereby although similarity is emphasized (a model of sameness), the similarity in question is immediately put in parenthesis, qualified by the admission of a difference. Hence, the aim of these kinds of articles in *Gringo*, which is to strip 'immigrants' of their difference, is in some sense undermined. The people in the articles are all positioned as 'other' even by being the object of investigation. The renegotiation of the social category in question works hand in hand with what the SIT tradition would call 'identification with the outgroup', or we could say, the identification with the ego-ideals of the Other. It is in terms of the identification with the ego-ideals of the Swedish big Other that the otherization of the immigrant can be understood. The 'Swedish' way of life seems to be taken for granted, seen as the background, the accepted backdrop against which examples of difference come to light and are particularized. What is considered to be the norm is communicated – the big Other of these texts is indirectly demonstrated in the images of difference. The big Other is Swedishness and from the position of the 'Swede' the immigrant needs to be represented, talked about and 'we' need to learn about 'them'.

We can sum up this section by stating that a 'social creativity' strategy in *Gringo* involves reversing the stereotypes of the immigrant, resisting images of difference, and making the immigrant more similar to the Swedish category. The ambivalence of this process, the insistence on difference, can be understood as a result of a conformity to the desire of the big Other of Swedish society. In the following I discuss a strategy in *Gringo* which does not involve reproducing, or conforming to, the ego-ideals of the Other. This is an attempt to make the immigrant recognizable on their 'own' terms, which means challenging the values embodied in the Swedish big Other.

Reinterpreting the 'inferior' characteristics of *blatte*

As stated above, *Gringo* makes use of the so-called *blatte* identity as a political category, and follows the trend already in progress in the Swedish media: the attempt to 'redeem' *blatte* or *svartskalle*, which involves reinterpreting their existing 'inferior' characteristics. This could be classified as Tajfel's strategy (ii) discussed in Chapter 6. It includes an attempt by *Gringo* to turn *blatte*, a negative term, into a positive one, by enhancing, even exaggerating, all the characteristics associated with this category. The idea here is to be 'proud' of being a *blatte*, looking like a *blatte*, or talking like a *blatte*, rather than being ashamed of it. Hence, the repeated use of the words *blatte* or *svartskalle* in the text of *Gringo* and the effort to make them 'everyday', ordinary words. Despite *Gringo*'s attempt, however, and despite the use of these words by many non-*Gringo* journalists often invited to write for the magazine, the words are still loaded. One 'external' author not part of the regular group of *Gringo* journalists writes the following extract. The author expresses her concerns over using such words:

> "I think it is a b ... b ... blatte thing". In the middle of a discussion, I test using The Prohibited Word ... I drip the word as cautiously as someone who takes a naked bath in February. Oooo how scary it is.
>
> (*Gringo* 23)

This indicates how the word *blatte* remains a tabooed term, how it is still considered offensive and prohibited in official, polite discourse. It suggests that the employment of the term in *Gringo* may not only be a social creativity strategy, an attempt to reinterpret its negative connotations. *Gringo* may wish to challenge the negative undertones of this word and disconnect it from the emotions that accompany it. As the quote above implies, however, *blatte* stays an emotional word. From a psychoanalytic perspective, that which is tabooed turns into an object of excitement. Prohibited objects evoke fascination and desire, and are associated with *jouissance*. We cannot therefore neglect the *jouissance* which may be involved in repetitively using a tabooed term, a *jouissance* which comes with transgression of social values and prohibitions regarding appropriateness.

Gringo's attempt to re-evaluate the *blatte* category is most evident in its promotion of *blatte-Swedish*. The following example demonstrates that *blatte-Swedish* may be a marker of a (proud) social identity, but it is *also* a transgression of Swedishness. The example is a comment by a *Gringo* reader (who could make comments in *Gringo* magazine and on its website). Many readers commented in *blatte-Swedish*, suggesting that there is a group who identify with this way of speaking. The following is an example:[9]

> Maaaaan, you're so daaamn cool!
>
> Hey all Gringo-people! One day I was sitting in the canteen eating when a teacher came to sit with us. We were talking and then I said "I'm crackin up". And my teacher said, "What are you saying? You should speak sensible Swedish". EEEEyyy maan, it's my damn free-time language! Stop complaining about how we talk. Not everybody is as perfect as you are. Hehe. We can talk in whatever way we want ... never talk proper Swede-language, blatte-Swedish is better :D I think your magazine is soo freakin cool. I started to read it when it was out in *Metro* and I can't wait for each new edition to come out. Damn, you're good. Keep it up! Your biggest fan, the blattis.
>
> (Dated 11 December 2006)

Ahmed (2004) states "emotionality of texts is one way of describing how texts are 'moving', or how they generate effects" (p. 13). Comments like the above demonstrate some of the effects that *Gringo's* text could have. Not only did the magazine contribute to the circulation of *blatte-Swedish* in the public arena, which could potentially challenge its stigmatization and subordinate position, but it also created a space where the representation or 'voicing' of *blatte-Swedish* could be legitimized. However, this comment also unveils the aversion or hostility towards this alternative way of speaking Swedish, and it illustrates that *blatte-Swedish* is after all seen as *opposite* to 'sensible Swedish'. Despite *Gringo's* attempt to make it *part* of the Swedish language, *blatte-Swedish* does not comfortably fit within the ambits of what, in the public imaginary, is considered 'correct' Swedish.

Anyone who is intentionally using *blatte-Swedish* is therefore at the same time expressing an identity and making a claim that he or she belongs to a certain social group and leads a specific way of life different to the 'norm' and the 'ordinary' lifestyle of a devoted Swede. The above example shows how identifying with the *blatte* category implies the externalization of the Swedish category. It could be read as a conscious identification with *blatte-Swedish*, and an unconscious alienation in the 'real Swede-language'. The latter is the Other of *blatte*, it is what is externalized, yet, being the repressed category, it is the very thing that 'holds' the being of *blatte* (see Pavón Cuéllar, 2010, p. 90). In other words, what we attribute to the Outgroup lies repressed within us, we are alienated in what we externalize to the Outgroup. The enthusiasm and thrill expressed in this example also conveys the enjoyment associated with the use of this deviant form of Swedish language, for it is precisely the awareness that one is breaking a norm connected with the Swedish language that brings about the elation of transgression. "The joy of transgression is an elation, an exuberance [and] it is in the slippage of rules and prohibitions, and simultaneously, the awareness of such slippage, that brings about [a] joyous experience" (Marchak, 1990, p. 361). Therefore, although the use of *blatte-Swedish* may indeed be an attempt to reinterpret its status as inferior, make it recognized as part of any other accent in Sweden, an effort to de-stigmatize it and make it commonplace in public discourse, it should not only be understood as a conscious resistance strategy. This is so because the use of *million-Swedish* appears to evoke some kind of enjoyment (for the author or for the reader of *Gringo* for instance). Taking into account the possible *jouissance* associated with *blatte-Swedish*, we can ask the following question: To what extent is *Gringo's* strategy a reinterpretation, and to what extent may it be a fetishization of the *blatte* category?

Reinterpretation or fetishism?

The re-evaluation of *blatte* includes the aim to change the image of the suburbs as 'dangerous' and 'shabby'. The function of the many articles in

Gringo that contain demographic, historical and 'factual' information about the suburbs is to turn these stigmatized and 'inferior' areas into ones with a recognized and distinctive history and identity. The descriptions of the suburbs are for the most part positive, depicting these areas as festive, diverse and trendy places, full of varied types of music, art and food. *Gringo* engages here in Tajfel's strategy (iii): introducing new group characteristics ('diversity' for instance) that have a positively valued distinctiveness to the superior group. The objective is clearly to make the suburbs visible, and to disrupt the negative connotations attributed to them by making them cheerful and exciting places. In order to do this, *Gringo* sometimes employs a mechanism of critique that the SIT paradigm fails to highlight (due to its disregard for language). This strategy entails ridiculing or making fun of stereotypical images. The following example is used to demonstrate how irony and satire in *Gringo* can have two functions at one and the same time: the 'conscious' aim is obviously to re-evaluate the *blatte* category, but what is not explicitly stated is how *blatte*, or a certain image of the suburb, is fetishized and enjoyed. The example is some extracts from a humorous and fictional 'survival guide' for the suburb:

Survival guide for the suburb

Gringo has created a survival guide for those who are courageous and want to go to the deadly suburb ...

Before you go:

- Visit the doctor to make sure that you're completely healthy. It's tough out there ...
- Take a course in first aid so you learn how to stitch gunshot wounds and knife-stabs on yourself
- Find out what gang-colours you need where you're going
- Write your will

How to behave:

- Try not to go alone. Bring a sidekick. Or a bodyguard is even better ...
- Don't show your bling-bling. Hide the mobile phone and everything else valuable ...
- If a car moves slowly with its windows down, you can be sure that it is a drive-by. Lie on the ground and play dead ...
- Don't ever say the words "yo mama" to anyone ...

Things to bring:

- Hair-colouring products: You can't browse around the suburb with some blond Dolph Lundgren hair-do. Everyone in the hood is dark-haired ...
- Bulletproof vest: A must in the suburb, no one leaves home without one ...

(*Gringo* 2)

According to *Gringo* the intention of this kind of inflated depiction is to show the absurdities in prejudices and stereotypes. As the editors state, "[We] take stereotypes and turn them around a few times in order to make visible all their absurdities" (*Gringo* 13). This statement suggests that the above exaggerated image is a way of criticizing and mocking the idea that the suburb is 'dangerous' and showing the nonsensical nature of this stereotype. We can see how the exaggerations and the humour can have the effect of critique, of showing the irrationalities or meaninglessness of stereotypes. This is typical of the 'Ali G style' critique, by which going over the top and eliciting laughter, the stereotypes are made ridiculous. It is similar to the transcoding strategy that Hall (1997) discusses, which, rather than changing its content, mainly involves working with the stereotype itself, with its *form*, in order to challenge it, de-familiarize it, and demonstrate its illogicality. It can also be argued that through humour, identities are made performative and contingent, which can be a challenge to stereotypes that represent identities as fixed.

With the use of hyperbole and sensational language, the stereotypes of the suburb are accentuated. The article's humorous and fictional form is not of little importance. The humour indicates that the aim is *not only* to critique, but also to incite laughter. The text is, moreover, enticing, it involves and engages us imaginatively, it draws attention, and it elicits a kind of voyeurism, indeed, even some form of prurience. The outcome of this type of 'critique' is then 'undecidable' in that even as one pretends to be critiquing a certain portrayal, one might still elicit obscene thrills, which can allow the reader to enjoy at a distance (and to cement a strong identification *against*) what is being objectified. This portrayal of the suburb can also be a prurient or vicarious *access* to the suburb. It gives answers to the question: 'what is it like in such places?' In the above extract, despite the fact that there is a distancing mechanism in place, by virtue of the use of parody, this mechanism allows us to enjoy at a remove; safe in the sense that this is joking discourse, we can nonetheless experience something of an imaginative 'thrill of the ghetto'.

However, the fiction also allows the reader to identify *with* this image; it can evoke a desire to *be* this image. The kind of language used in this piece of text is very common in *Gringo*. The slang and the use of North American English words (for example, the suburb is referred to as 'the hood') can evoke an identification with the African American vernacular style of speaking. This article, and numerous other similar texts in *Gringo* about 'gangster' figures in African American movies and music, indicates a *fascination* with the 'gangster' or 'ghetto' image. While the exaggerated image of the suburb as 'dangerous', 'violent', or as similar to the African American 'hoods' may be a strong parody and critique of stereotypes, it can also be read as a desire for narratives that transgress Swedish cultural laws of 'normalcy' or 'decency'.

We can therefore assume that there may be a *disavowal* occurring here: we *know* that stereotypes are not true, but we still *believe*, or *feel* them as if they are true. For Freud (1927) the refusal to accept a certain uncomfortable reality or knowledge (for example, the 'stereotypes are not true') includes disavowal of this knowledge ('I don't want to know that stereotypes are not true'). The denial of a reality leaves a gap and a need to fill that gap with a fetish object. In psychoanalysis, *the fetish proves that something is not so*. This object becomes very important to the subject because it conceals the gap, and it helps the subject to 'forget' about it. However, the fetish object is also a reminder of the gap. Therefore, paradoxically this object represents both the disavowal of reality and its acknowledgement. It represents both anxiety and pleasure. It is the ambivalence of anxiety and pleasure which requires the fetish object to be repetitively evoked; it needs a repetition of action in order to make sure that the threatening idea which brings about anxiety is covered over. It needs to provide a certain kind of fixity. The more I repeat it, the more I establish to myself that something is not the case, because I have the fetish object to prove it. If the fetish is in evidence, continually resorted to, then the sort of identity that would otherwise be threatened can be maintained, and ensures that a narcissistic *jouissance* can be protected and assured.

In the text of *Gringo*, the exaggerated image of the suburb as 'dangerous', 'violent', the ideas of 'difference', which come up again and again, might indeed be a strategy that involves making the stereotypes absurd, an effort to re-evaluate *blatte*. However, it can also be read as a repeated fetishized representation. The *blatte*/ghetto identity is almost like a piece of clothing that people can wear in order to project a more desirable image of themselves. In this sense, we can say that the *blatte* identity is like a commodity fetish, the commodity (*blatte*/ghetto identity) is filled with fetish qualities, and it is worshipped for the ability to provide *jouissance*. Just like products such as shoes or cars, the *blatte*/ghetto identity is a fetish object which is imagined to assure fulfilment.

So, what exactly is threatening about the idea 'stereotypes are not true'? The beginning of this chapter showed how *Gringo* attempts to make the immigrant 'normal' and just like any other 'ordinary' Swede, similar to the Swede. It might be the idea of *sameness, homogeneity or lack of difference* which proves threatening, because it means that I am just like anybody else. SIT in many ways recognizes this 'need' to see oneself as 'different' (e.g. Tajfel, 1978, 1981, p. 337). From Lacanian theory we learn how this 'need' is associated with anxiety, with the gaze of the Other and with a libidinal sense of enjoyment. Being seen in the gaze of the Other as different provides me with a sense of distinctiveness, a kind of affirmation of specialness; the feeling of difference provides *jouissance*. 'No difference' might itself be a threatening idea; it is a threat to the *jouissance* which comes with difference. *Blatte* as the fetish object is the object/monument that keeps difference alive and denies complete sameness. Here it helps to refer back to an earlier analytical observation: that there is no room for the immigrant to be positively visible except by taking up a place within the ambit of the home culture's ego-ideals, as governed by the Other. One would expect then that some images would play into these ego-ideals, but also that there would be some attempt to resist them, to deny this homogenization, and assert an identity able to evince a degree of difference. In other words, this example of a fetishistic resort to ensure a threatened identity should be seen as dynamically related to the foregoing ego-ideal-harmonizing identities. It provides a crucial way of ensuring a different mode of identity against the threatening homogenization of the ego-ideals of the Swedish Other; it keeps a threatened identity alive and secure, and enables its own particular type of *jouissance* into the bargain.

To summarize, this depiction of the suburb may be seen as a challenge to stereotypes, part of the attempt to reinterpret the negative aspects of the *blatte* image, but it can also be read as *resistance to (and alienation in) the ego-ideals of the big Other*; a resistance to be what the Other wants me to be. Therefore, we could state that the fetishization of the *blatte* category involves a transgression of Swedishness, and from the repeated and almost theatrical mode of expression – both in the 'guide' to the suburb and in the reader's comment above – we can argue that there may be a *jouissance* involved in this transgression.

Reinterpreting the blatte category means changing the symbolic

Tajfel argues that it is often externally imposed categories that contribute to the development of a sense of separate identity within a minority group: "once this happens, a minority enters a spiral of psychological separateness in which the 'outside' social categorizations are associated with their 'inside' acceptance by the group in a mutually reinforcing convergence" (Tajfel, 1981, p. 314). People labelled as, for example, 'immigrant' or '*blatte*' never chose to call themselves as such. These categories are in fact *signifiers* imposed by the Other. They are designated by the Other to point out, denote and exemplify, that which is different and transgresses the norm and the acceptable. Therefore, when acting in terms of the *blatte* category, for example, one acts to a considerable extent in terms of the Other. This also implies, logically speaking, that it does not make sense to 'redeem' or 'take back' *blatte* because it never belonged to the supposed members of this category in the first place: it is a signifier of the Other – albeit one that designates that which is disgraceful and discreditable.

The search for positive distinctiveness in *Gringo*, the attempt to make the *blatte* category acceptable and legitimized, involves *changing* Swedishness itself. It entails transforming those signifiers that are prioritized by the Swedish Other. In the following extracts it is suggested that the Swedish name day calendar should become "*blatte-fied*".

> Are you tired of your *Svenne* name? It is more common than you think and nothing to be ashamed of. You can just change it. You can now blatte-fy your name without betraying your origins ... If your name is something incredibly common such as Rebecka, you can change it to a luxurious Asian name, such as Ping, or to something foxy, like Felicity ... The Swedish calendar, just like the rest of the country, has not kept up with the new Swedishness. It is about time that, for example, the 190 Ringvalds[10] disappear and leave space for the over 5700 Alis...
>
> (*Gringo* 12)

We could argue that this is a type of *social comparison* strategy where the ingroup (those with foreign names) is favoured, and the outgroup (those with Swedish names) is negatively discriminated against. This method simultaneously re-appraises the devalued *blatte* category. However, it would be simplistic to view the outgroup in such terms. This is more than a straightforward instance of outgroup discrimination. The Swedish name day calendar, is rooted in, and reflects, a Swedish cultural and religious institution; it stands for the symbolic Other. Hence, we should understand this text as being about a relationship to the socio-symbolic field of Swedish society. The proposal to include Muslim names such as Ali, a signifier of something essentially non-Swedish, would otherwise be considered as threatening to the name day calendar. It would alter the calendar radically if Ali was part of it. The above text suggests therefore an antinomy, an impasse of wanting to be included in the Swedish symbolic history, yet at the same time to retain those qualities inimical to it, which would fundamentally modify this tradition. Making *blatte* a positively evaluated category should thus be understood as an effort to change the symbolic. In other words, the *blatte category could not be positively evaluated without changing the ego-ideals* – those ideals of the big Other which determine what is and is not a 'positive' category.

Gringo's attempt to change the symbolic is most evident in its promotion of *blatte-Swedish*. For example, one section in *Gringo* is called *Nya svenska ord* (New Swedish words). Words from languages spoken in the suburbs, such as Turkish, Arabic, Persian or Spanish, are introduced here and their meanings are explained. *Gringo's* use of the 'slang' spoken by youth in the suburbs is a larger attempt to make this way of speaking Swedish recognized as *part* of the Swedish language, and not its opposite, not something which signifies that which is not Swedish. *Gringo* calls this accent *miljon-svenska* (million-Swedish). According to the magazine, it was one of the editors who came up with the aforementioned term. The argument is that "it is the best term because it suggests that the language is geographically linked to the Million Programme areas and does not exclude *svenne*[11] [Swedes] and at the same time it doesn't include all blattes" (*Gringo* 22). Thus, *Gringo* prides itself on taking the initiative to "define [Swedish] culture" (*Gringo* 22). However, as we will see below, the use of *blatte-Swedish* in *Metro*, a widely available media source, was not received without criticism in the Swedish public sphere. The publication of a series of articles in *Gringo* about the Swedish language is a response to these criticisms. The function of these articles is to defend *Gringo's* use of *million-Swedish*, challenge the negative connotations of this way of speaking, remove the stigma attached to it, and make it accepted by the symbolic. The following extract is from an article in the editorial section. The author states that he is no longer ashamed of his *blatte-Swedish*:

> Today I can be ashamed for being ashamed. Or not ashamed, but look back and think, it was a bloody pity that it had to be that way. Just like everyone else, I had an image of the million-Swedish I was speaking as ugly. An ugly dialect used by ugly people. Something I had to wash away if I wanted to be successful. Today, newspapers, companies and teachers who don't appreciate million-Swedish lose points in my eyes. And I will never in my life work for a company that thinks million-Swedish is bad Swedish.
>
> (*Gringo* 22)

The pressure of being 'Swedish' and 'normal', the demand to adhere to the ego-ideals of the symbolic field of the Other, are resisted passionately. But here is not a matter of a wish to maintain a distinctive, self-enclosed way of life; there is no claim for a separate linguistic community. On the contrary, the demand is to be recognized as part of a wider Swedish symbolic community, while maintaining the distinctive qualities of *blatte-Swedish*. Of course, making *million-Swedish* legitimized would mean transforming the Swedish language itself. As predicted by SIT, *Gringo's* attempt to change the Swedish language was received by some as a serious threat to the perception of Swedishness as 'superior'. Indeed, following SIT, we could state that a response to this sense of threat was the endeavour to reaffirm the supremacy of the Swedish language.

Enhancing the distinctiveness of the Swedish language

There were of course both positive and negative reactions to *Gringo* magazine in the Swedish public sphere, but it was the negative ones, especially in relation to the Swedish language, which were most passionately expressed. The Swedish language became a topic of public debate, particularly in Sweden's largest morning newspaper, *Dagens Nyheter*. This debate was also replicated in *Gringo's* editorial and other sections, where the use of *blatte-Swedish* was defended, and where the idea of the Swedish language as untainted and pure was criticized.

Even though *Gringo* was not the first to introduce the so-called *blatte-Swedish* to the media, the use of this slang language in the text of the magazine and *Gringo's* aim to introduce new foreign words into the Swedish language caused controversy in some segments of the Swedish society. The slang language of *Gringo* and the 'misuse' of the Swedish language was one of the main issues which evoked strong defensive reactions by the public. This indicates that it is in its threat to the Swedish language that *Gringo* was perhaps most subversive. We will examine this idea.

The increased use of *blatte-Swedish* in the media led to an ever more heated public debate about the status of the Swedish language. In 2006 the subject of the Swedish language became such a popular topic that the anti-racism programme called *Nollrasism* (Zero racism) on *TV4*, one of Sweden's largest TV channels, focused on the Swedish language as the theme of that year's programme. Elsewhere, a debate was stirred up with the introduction of two words derived from the suburbs, *keff* (lousy, shitty) and *guss* (chick), in the 2006 version of the *Svenska akademiens ordlista* (Swedish Academic Wordlist). This introduction of *blatte-Swedish* into a wordlist highly regarded as the symbolic container of Swedishness led to fierce emotional responses.

Not specifically referring to *Gringo*, the use of *blatte-Swedish* was criticized in 2006 by Ebba Witt-Brattström, a professor in Swedish literature, in a debate on TV. She argued that the government, rather than focusing on mother tongue education,[12] should encourage the teaching of Swedish to immigrants, and not give the message that knowing only *blatte-Swedish* was sufficient to cope in society; and it should promote the learning of Swedish so that people with immigration backgrounds would face less discrimination in the labour market (Witt-Brattström, 2006b).

A debate was stirred up in *Dagens Nyheter*, where major public figures, including Witt-Brattström and *Gringo's* editorial, were defending or attacking the use of *million-Swedish*, the teaching of mother tongues in schools, and the status of the Swedish language. The debate became intense and began to extend to other topics such as the link between *blatte-Swedish* and sexism. The core of this discussion seemed, however, to surround the topic of Swedishness.

In one of her articles, Witt-Brattström criticized *Gringo's* use of *million-Swedish* and called it a "media-bluff" and a "marketing-concept" (Witt-Brattström, 2006a). This is what she stated about the suburb language:

> The standard language is Swedish, and its importance as a communication tool is also fundamental for new Swedes. The multi-slang is not an alternative ... To advocate a school that takes seriously the role of Swedish as important in society does not mean to be against mother tongue education, or for that matter against other important languages within our immediate geographical context ... Multilingualism is good, but Swedish is the basis for everything because we live in Sweden, and only literate people can fully participate in society.
>
> (Witt-Brattström, 2006a)

As SIT recognizes, a threat to the superiority of a group requires the production of distinctive symbols in order to maintain the perception of superiority (Tajfel, 1981). Witt-Brattström attempts to preserve the image of the Swedish language as essential, distinctive and necessarily superior. The text expresses a *fantasy* of Swedish language as something that is somehow pure, uncontaminated and primary, and potentially threatened by an alternative slang language. Very similar criticisms to Witt-Brattström's arguments could be found in comments made by *Gringo's* readers. A great deal of the remarks implied that *Gringo* was a threat to the Swedish way of life and to Swedish people. Many perceived the discussions in *Gringo* about Swedish culture and new Swedishness as being 'anti-Sweden'. This was particularly so with regards to the use (or for some – the *abuse*) of the Swedish language. Many of the comments referred to *million-Swedish* and – as one of the commentators put it – "the destruction of the Swedish language" (dated 1 April 2007). This is one example:

> You're part of the aim by the Swedish left to weaken Swedish culture and the Swedish language. You're a big bluff by claiming that a million

immigrants want to talk your bluff language. You're simply bluff-blattes. Everybody apart from the media has already seen through you. How long do you think that you can go on before people get sick of you? Laissez faire, et dire.

(Dated 29 May 2006)

It is likely that this person has read Witt-Brattström's article (which was published before the date of this comment), and one could say that it reverberates a fierier version of Witt-Brattström's voice. *Gringo* is considered to threaten a 'precious' Swedishness. Other comments include similar images of threat:

> Bloody hell. I become dead-anxious when I see that you're raping the Swedish language. You don't seem to want to be here in Sweden and adapt to our culture, but you should not think that you could rule in whatever way you want and moan about Swedes being racists. End the bullshit and grow up. Halstatt nordid.
>
> (Dated 20 February 2007)

These are passionate comments and they demonstrate an anxiety about *Gringo* being a danger to the Swedish way of life. *Gringo's* challenge to the Swedish language and Swedishness, and its attempt to change a seemingly unchanging symbolic order, are viewed by some as a threat to something that is highly emotionally charged. What is it about the Swedish language which means that any attempt to challenge it and alter it is felt to be so frightening? Why are the responses to *million-Swedish* so full of affect, so defensive and 'paranoid'? We cannot look to SIT for answers to these questions, because although it acknowledges that an 'insecure' identity will lead the superior group to 'search for distinctiveness', it does not tell us why this search is often an intensely passionate process.

From a psychoanalytic perspective, the passionate responses to *Gringo's* perceived threat suggest that the Swedish language is part of a fantasy frame. In this fantasy, the Swedish language is the source of *jouissance*; it is the 'Thing' fantasized to offer *jouissance*. This means that any threat to the language is also a threat to the particularity of one's *jouissance*. As stated in Chapter 4, a community is sustained by virtue of certain 'properties'. These properties are those aspects of a community that represent its distinctiveness – these can be myths, legends, language, cultural rituals – anything that defines 'who we are' and which has been given the quality of a precious object and invested with narcissistic enjoyment. We know from Chapter 4 that Žižek (1993) calls these features of a community and the *jouissance* which they are believed to provide, the Thing: "National identification is by definition sustained by a relationship towards the Nation qua Thing" (Žižek, 1993, p. 201). It is the Thing which makes us who we are and sustains our community. The Thing can, however, never be completely represented, it can "only [be] alluded to" (Daly, 1999, p. 228).

The property, the Thing which is at stake in the above, is alluded to in the Swedish language. Swedish language, a national tool loaded with narcissism, is viewed as a specific, irreplaceable attribute of Swedishness. It is one of 'our' qualities that make us special – alongside our culture, our children, our way of life – and it gives us *jouissance*. The above comments by readers – which demonstrate feelings of persecution – express a fear that one's *jouissance* is being unjustly threatened. *Gringo* with its *blatte-Swedish* is blamed by some readers for contaminating and thus depriving the nation of its *jouissance*, its bodily enjoyment. The remarks point to the anxiety that one's National Thing (Swedish language), and the *jouissance* linked to it, is being spoiled by *blatte-Swedish* – something radically other and dirty. There is a fear here of the Other contaminating our language with their own ways of speaking, their own *jouissance*. As Žižek (1993) states, the feeling is that "he [in this case *Gringo*] wants to steal our enjoyment (by ruining our way of life)" (p. 203). In short, we could state that:

- Gringo is believed to be threatening Swedish language with its own strange, odd way of speaking;
- It is the *jouissance of blatte-Swedish* spoken by them, which is unbearable.

The other's *jouissance* is intolerable because it is a token of the disgust of our own excessive enjoyment (Žižek, 1993).

Gringo's transgressive language represents excessive, unbearable enjoyment which needs to be eliminated because it does not conform to the imaginary unity, the ego-ideals of Swedishness. The last two comments above made by *Gringo* readers may express the *jouissance* involved in problematizing this 'foreign' mode of *Gringo's jouissance*, and could perhaps be seen as unsanctioned versions of Witt-Brattström's official and authorized discourse. The examples nonetheless demonstrate a fantasy in which a 'pure' Swedish language, untainted by *Gringo's* 'bluff' Swedish, is what would permit ultimate purification or what Daly (1999) calls "the realisation of harmonious reconciliation" (p. 224). Accordingly, the fantasy goes something like this: 'if it wasn't for *Gringo* and its *blatte*-language, we would retain that treasured, lost Thing'. What is paradoxical, however, is that the Thing, or *jouissance*, can never be obtained. The Thing exists only insofar as it has been threatened. Thus, "what we conceal by imputing to the Other the theft of enjoyment is the traumatic fact that we never possessed what was allegedly stolen from us" (Žižek, 1993, p. 203).

To sum up, *Gringo* managed to upset a fantasy relation to 'standard Swedish' as the superior Thing. Whether *Gringo* had a more significant effect than that is questionable. It is not necessarily the case that *Gringo* succeeded in challenging the deep emotional investment in 'standard-Swedish'. It would be more accurate to state that it merely managed to offend a rigid fantasy. As the examples above suggest, although the fantasy of the 'pure' Swedish language might have been unmasked and slightly shaken up, it could be asked whether it was made even stronger by portraying *Gringo* as the threat. *Gringo* may have become the Other responsible for the loss of the Thing. One can therefore ask whether the magazine could have in fact contributed to strengthening the narcissistic fantasy of Swedishness as superior. With the advent of *Gringo* and its threatening transgressive language, the fantasy of Swedish language needed to be defended, affirmed and fortified. Hence, it is through embodying *Gringo* as the blameworthy villain who poses a threat that a fantasy can be sustained in which the Swedish language is alluded to as the Thing promising salvation.

Conclusion

Our discussion of *Gringo* demonstrates that social creativity strategies should be understood as a matter of desire. Discursive approaches that analyse how categories are renegotiated in discourse, via, for example, rhetoric, are therefore inadequate. They are not interested in anything beyond discourse and therefore ignore issues of desire and enjoyment. This chapter has shown how the search for distinctiveness or social identity is fundamentally related to *jouissance*. The re-evaluation of *blatte* is a transgression of Swedishness, an identification with the image of 'difference', which is fantasized to bring about *jouissance*. The attempt to preserve the distinctiveness of the Swedish language as a response to the threat of *blatte-Swedish* is an effort to defend the Thing. In other words, *a perceived threat to identity is a threat to jouissance*, which is an important reason why this threat often ends up in passionate and sometimes (or often) bloody conflict. *Gringo*'s threat to Swedishness did not, however, lead to any significant conflict, apart from heated debates in some segments of the public sphere. The examples in this chapter nevertheless allude to the *jouissance* that is often at stake in social conflict.

Tajfel (1981) states that a determining factor when a subordinated group re-evaluates its existing 'inferior' qualities is whether "the others acknowledge the new image, separate but equal or superior, on consensually-valued dimensions?" (p. 286). *Gringo*'s image of *blatte* as a distinctive and valued category was not well received by many segments of the Swedish society. Nor was it accepted by many individuals with immigration backgrounds

(*Gringo* had many critics who were first- or second-generation immigrants), which we could understand as part of the reasons why it ultimately failed to make *blatte* a positive source for identity.

Gringo was a magazine that not only transgressed the Swedish symbolic, linguistic and ideological rules and laws, but it was also one which resisted accepted journalistic norms. It presented itself as anomalous to mainstream journalism in Sweden, a context where irony and humour are rare, perceived as 'deviant', and often misunderstood in political discourse. Of course, this could be one of the reasons why the magazine experienced a reduction in audience, and why it eventually had to be terminated. However, as we know, the more something is socially outlawed, the more it is desired. There *was* after all a great amount of enthusiasm around *Gringo* and it was very popular, especially in the first few years of its inception. In 2005 Adami was even awarded the prestigious Bonnier journalism prize for founding it, and some praised the magazine for its success in subverting stereotypes and promoting a heterogeneous notion of Swedishness (e.g. Alarcón, 2008). A Lacanian perspective allows us, nevertheless, to explore the possibility that the function of *Gringo* may not solely have been social critique or social change, as SIT would presume. What if the promotion of difference may not above all demonstrate a rejection of the status quo? Lacanian theory offers us the tools to explore other possible functions of the magazine in the public sphere: perhaps its main (intended or unintended) task was to organize or administrate temporary experience of *jouissance*, a *jouissance* that is not only covertly or overtly prohibited in the Swedish cultural context, but also despised.

8 Conclusions

Concepts derived from psychoanalysis, a discipline dismissed by the SIT tradition, have been used in this book to deconstruct and rework this tradition. As Brown and Lunt (2002) imply, however, despite being averse to psychoanalysis, the SIT paradigm in fact secretly *relies* on Freudian theory. Indeed, the central concept of this paradigm, the concept of identification, *originates* in psychoanalysis. In Freudian and Lacanian psychoanalysis, identification is understood as a mostly unconscious, and a primarily *affective* process at the heart of the constitution of subjectivity. By identifying with an image or a signifier, the subject becomes a social subject, a member of a community. In Lacanian theory, identification does not mean identity. Becoming identical to, the same as, someone else is an impossibility even though we never stop trying to achieve a sense of eternal 'oneness'. The SIT approach, especially in its recent form, has taken the very complicated notion of identification from psychoanalysis, transformed it into a cognitive process, and renamed it 'self-categorization'. Whereas the psychoanalytic notion of identification de-centres the subject, turns the subject into something Other than him or her 'self', the SIT paradigm endows the subject with a 'self' and with essential qualities such as rational and cognitive powers.

Despite these problems, rather than an outright dismissal of the SIT approach, this book has taken its main ideas and demonstrated how they could be reworked with Lacanian theory. The attempt has not been to combine the two theories, but to use one as a method in order to rethink the other. Moreover, it should be mentioned again that the aim has *not* been to offer a complete theory of identity, group and intergroup relations. Such a task is impossible given that each case of group and intergroup relation is different from another and must be analysed independently in its specific historical context. What this book has highlighted are issues that are explicitly absent from the SIT framework, even though they may often be implicit in this framework. These are issues of desire, fantasy and affect. These elements of subjectivity *cannot* be ruled out in any social psychological theory of identity, group and intergroup relations. We have seen that once these aspects of subjectivity are included in the picture, some of the ideas of the SIT tradition become deeply problematic. Group and intergroup relations become, not a matter of cognition or perception, but of the symbolic and *jouissance*. As discursive psychologists have rightly pointed out, one of the most serious failings of the social identity approach is its lack of concern with language. Relations between and within groups (just like human relations in general) are fundamentally linguistic and symbolic relations. They are essentially a relation between signifiers. Intergroup conflict is, at its most basic level, a conflict between signifiers, between 'Hutus' and 'Tutsis', 'Arabs' and 'Jews', 'Khadafi-supporters' and 'Rebels'. Humans are often willing to die for the signifier, and are therefore, in many ways, not much more than the support and agent of the signifier (see Pavón Cuéllar, 2010, p. 124). From our Lacanian perspective, categories are not simply cognitive structures. They are symbolic elements that structure and determine the "'objective' competition" (Tajfel, 1981, p. 251) between groups. From this perspective, the symbolic *is* the objective. Signifiers are material.

As we have seen, however, both intra- and intergroup relations contain a bodily aspect that cannot easily be accommodated within the symbolic. Signifiers (i.e. categories) are often affectively loaded, they evoke and manage *jouissance*. Intergroup conflict and social change are more than matters of cognition, knowledge, judgement, or discourse. A Lacanian approach shows us that the power of the symbolic in the mobilization of *jouissance* does not only function to maintain or stabilize a certain social relation between groups, but it also drives the transformation of these relations. For example, cultural discursive products, such as literature, can work to not only delegitimize existing power structures, but they can also contribute to the instability of these structures. How can these products have this effect? As we saw in Chapter 2, Reicher and Hopkins (1996, 2001a, 2001b) imply that discourse and rhetorical methods are often used to change people's perception of the world, mobilize people and facilitate action. These authors highlight the role of identities as defined in discourse, in enabling (or inhibiting) action. However, they do not consider that discourse can mobilize groups of people because they manage to call upon, or evoke some *desire*. Therefore, those aiming to induce collective action do not only have to be "entrepreneurs of identity" (Reicher & Hopkins, 2001a, p. 387), but also 'entrepreneurs of desire'. Social movements are often inspired by political literature and art that produce new terms and terminologies (i.e. signifiers) with which to conceive the world, and new desires. Fanon, for example, understood the role of literature as fundamental in the nationalist anti-colonial struggle. This is

the literature of combat, in the sense that it calls on the whole people to fight for their existence as a nation. It is a literature of combat, because it moulds the national consciousness, giving it form and contours and flinging open before it new and boundless horizons; it is a literature of combat because it assumes responsibility, and because it is the will to liberty expressed in terms of time and space.

(Fanon, 1990, p. 193)

Such literature uses language that manages to not only create cognitive alternatives, but also a possible shift in desire. Today's modern communication technology has played a significant role in creating and spreading cognitive alternatives, and destabilizing and delegitimizing systems of power. Modern mass media distributes images and signifiers that people from geographically separate locations can identify with, and thus create the possibilities for change. For example, the media facilitated the spread of the 2011 demonstrations across the Arab and Muslim world when it distributed images of protest against dictatorship in one Arab country, and thereby created cognitive alternatives in another Arab country. We shall note here that these technologies would not in *themselves* facilitate these movements. Communication technologies would not be effective if it was not for certain subjective factors, such as identification and desire. Indeed, media technology would be unsuccessful in mobilizing groups if it was not for the mechanism of identification. Masses in geographically disparate locations all over the world have been able to congregate around and identify with the signifier 'Arab', and engage in action against their oppressors. Some discourses, signifiers and images "can prompt us to feel or act in certain ways and [they] can also re-form or alter our foundational, structural identifications and thus change our subjectivity and our behaviour as well" (Bracher, 1993, p. 22). Discourses that manage to alter our position are those that coerce us to give up our desires, and/or assume new ones. *Identity works to enable or limit action because it works on desire.* "When an identification becomes established as our identity, it functions to repress all desires that are incongruent with this identity" (Bracher, 1993, p. 22). Discourse includes signifiers and images that evoke and direct desires. In order to make an impact, 'external' signifiers will point to the subjects' 'internal' sense of being. The effect of discourse in making a change and transforming subjectivity derives from the fact that one's desire is put at stake.

Let us stress, however, that change is a defining aspect of modern multicultural and consumerist societies. Social change is *immanent* in today's capitalism. "Capitalism possesses a remarkable ability to alter reality radically and revolutionize itself constantly" (Stavrakakis, 2007, p. 168). Our times differ from Tajfel's when social movements towards the recognition of, for example, black people and women had only just taken off properly. Today, multiculturalist policies are based on the assumption that different religions, 'races', or ethnicities, are not inferior. Consumer society even encourages hybrid, alternative identities, and promotes the transgression of traditional norms. Capitalist discourse constantly calls on us to be innovative, to reinforce our uniqueness, to stand out and to be different. In some ways, therefore, the SIT paradigm's 'search for distinctiveness' illustrates well this capitalist worldview. Many social movements and 'identity politics' are today commercial. They conform to the demands of the market. Images of identity can turn into cultural productions available for consumption, and as some Lacanian theorists argue, *jouissance* is at the centre of capitalist consumption (e.g. Böhm & Batta, 2010). When *jouissance* is taken seriously we do not unquestionably celebrate all collective actions that at first sight appear to be designed for change. This is because the desire for change and the desire for *jouissance* may be entangled together, making it in some cases difficult to ascertain what exactly motivates action.

Our discussions in this book raise a question about the extent to which theories in social psychology could or should 'describe' social behaviour without participating in social analysis and critique. The SIT approach seeks to explain and predict social and political behaviour, not to change it. This is typical of mainstream social psychology where "abstract characterization of political behavior evacuates political analysis" (Parker, 2007, p. 27). One of the aims of the critical approach to psychology is to construct theories and concepts that help to not simply understand social behaviour, but also to criticize it and change it when it is deemed damaging or oppressive in various ways. For example, rather than aiming to predict when subordinated groups will reject their subordination and engage in collective struggle (prediction is in any case ultimately impossible), our analysis could focus on criticizing those struggles that may be counter-productive, and suggest alternative approaches. Various theories and concepts could be used to help identify such alternative approaches, and psychoanalysis is one of them. For example, some political theorists use Lacanian ideas about subjective change in the clinical setting to consider political change. This is not so straightforward though, as one cannot simply apply knowledge derived from the clinical psychoanalytic situation where individuals may be clinically induced to abandon their destructive patterns of behaviour, to suggest changes at the collective level in the socio-political field. Lacanian theory does, however, include certain useful ideas about change that may help us to begin to think about what a more viable 'social change belief structure' would look like.

What is particularly valuable about psychoanalysis is its deep concern with questions of why people cling to ideas or behaviours that are destructive, and what a more 'real' rejection of such behaviours would imply. From this perspective a feasible change strategy would imply a dis-identification with, for example, capitalist endorsement of 'difference'. This would entail the 'undoing' of identifications with group images, signifiers and discourses that are unprogressive and which reproduce capitalist or other modes of exploitation and inequality. Psychoanalysis teaches us that change at a cognitive level, in our perception of the world, needs to be accompanied by change in libidinal economy. As we know, people are libidinally attached to discourse, "attachments that are often resistant to criticism and change" (Stavrakakis, 2007, p. 163). A Lacanian approach to social change would emphasize that "real change requires not the discursive production of new knowledge but as certain mobility in desire" (Alcorn, 2002, p. 98). Therefore, 'real' change is when there has been a change in the way in which groups experience *jouissance* (see Glynos & Stavrakakis, 2003, p. 125). Change means a change in relation to our *jouissance*; it means the removal of the libidinal investments we make in signifiers of identity. Of course, it is not clear how exactly such transformation in *jouissance* would take place at a collective level, or whether it is even possible to get groups of people to adopt such a reflective approach to their own enjoyment, in the same manner as perhaps individuals could after years in clinical psycho-analysis. Again, each case of intergroup relations must be examined in its historical context, and psychoanalytic theory may or may not be useful, and could perhaps be combined with other approaches, depending on the type and aim of the analysis. Indeed, psychoanalytic theory may contain valuable concepts that could be used to analyse, theorize and even subvert groups and intergroup relations, but it is not a perfect theory, it does not have all the answers – even though it offers a worthwhile alternative to social psychology.

Notes

1 Hogg and Abrams (1988) view the SIT and the self-categorization theory (SCT) as part of the same framework. Therefore, in this book, terms such as the 'SIT tradition', 'SIT paradigm', or 'SIT approach' refer to the whole tradition of intergroup and intragroup research (thus, SIT and SCT combined). SIT refers to the branch about intergroup relations. SCT stands for the branch concerning ingroup processes as developed in Turner et al. (1987).

2 When discussing the minimal group experiments, this chapter follows Tajfel and colleagues in using the term 'subject' to refer to participants in a psychological experiment.

3 Although a 'fair' distribution of points was considered another important result of the experiments, it has been ignored in the later discussions and in the elaboration of the SIT as a whole (see Condor, 2003).

4 The text from *Gringo* seen in this chapter has been translated from Swedish to English by the author of this book.

5 '*Gringo* 18' stands for *Gringo* edition number 18. As part of a larger research that was conducted between 2005 and 2009, most of *Gringo's* online editions and a large number of comments made by *Gringo's* readers were downloaded and saved in 2007 from the now defunct *Gringo* website: Gringo.se. If required, this material can be obtained from the author of this book.

6 Rinkeby and Rosengård are suburbs in the outskirts of Stockholm and Malmö where a high number of residents are refugees or first-, second- and third-generation immigrants.

7 Due to limitations of space this chapter only includes extracts from *Gringo* and not full articles. See Dashtipour (2009) for the complete articles.

8 *Bo* and *Leif* are traditional and common Scandinavian names.

9 Note that it is not a straightforward matter to translate *blatte-Swedish* into English. In spite of the challenges of translation, every attempt has been made to do justice to what is being expressed in the Swedish text.

10 *Ringvald* is an old-fashioned Swedish name.

11 *Svenne* is an offensive term referring to 'native' Swedes – an analogy is the English 'whitey'. As well as *blatte*, Gringo frequently uses *svenne* in an attempt to abolish its negative connotations.

12 Teaching mother tongue to pupils with immigration backgrounds is part of the school curriculum in Sweden.

Bibliography

Adorno, T.W., Fenkel-Brunswik, E., Levinson, D.J., & Stanford, R.N. (1950). *The authoritarian personality*. New York: Harper.

Ahmed, S. (2004). *The cultural politics of emotion*. Edinburgh: Edinburgh University Press.

Alarcón Alanes, P.A. (2008). Konturer av motstånd: Identitet, subjektivitet och språk i tidningen Gringo. *Nordicom-Information*, 30(1), 55–66.

Alcorn, M.W. (1994). The subject of discourse: Reading Lacan through (and beyond) poststructuralist contexts. In Bracher, M., Alcorn, M.W., Corthell, R.J., & Massardier-Kenney, F. (Eds.), *Lacanian theory of discourse: Subject, structure and society* (pp. 19–45). New York: New York University Press.

Alcorn, M.W. (2002). *Changing the subject in English class: Discourse and the constructions of desire*. Carbondale: Southern Illinois University Press.

Ålund, A., & Schierup, C.U. (1991). *Paradoxes of multiculturalism*. Aldershot: Avebury.

Augoustinos, M., & Reynolds, K.J. (2001). *Understanding prejudice, racism and social conflict*. London: Sage.

Augoustinos, M., Tuffin, K., & Rapley, M. (1999). Genocide or a failure to gel? Racism, history and nationalism in Australian talk. *Discourse & Society*, 10, 351–378.

Augoustinos, M., & Walker, I. (1995). *Social cognition: An integrated introduction*. London: Sage.

Berkowitz, N.H. (1994). Evidence that subject's expectations confound intergroup bias in Tajfel's minimal group paradigm. *Personality and Social Psychology Bulletin*, 20, 184–195.

Billig, M. (1973). Normative communication in a minimal intergroup situation. *European Journal of Social Psychology*, 3(3), 339–343.

Billig, M. (1985). Prejudice, categorisation and particularisation: From a perceptual to a rhetorical approach. *European Journal of Social Psychology*, 15, 79–103.

Billig, M. (1996). Remembering the particular background of social identity theory. In Robinson, W.P. (Ed.), *Social groups and identities: Developing the legacy of Henri Tajfel* (pp. 337–357). Oxford: Butterworth-Heinemann.

Billig, M. (1997). Rhetorical and discursive analysis: How families talk about the royal family. In Hayes, N. (Ed.), *Introduction to qualitative methods* (pp. 39–54). Hove, Sussex: Lawrence Erlbaum.

Billig, M. (2002). Henri Tajfel's 'cognitive aspects of prejudice' and the psychology of bigotry. *British Journal of Social Psychology*, 41, 171–188.

Billig, M., & Tajfel, H. (1973). Social categorization and similarity in intergroup behavior. *European Journal of Social Psychology*, 3, 27–52.

Blank, H. (1997). Cooperative participants discriminate (not always): A logic of conversation approach to the minimal group paradigm. *Current Issues in Social Psychology*, 2(5), 38–49.

Böhm, S., & Batta, A. (2010). Just doing it: Enjoying commodity fetishism with Lacan. *Organization*, 17(3), 345–361.

Bracher, M. (1993). *Lacan discourse and social change: A psychoanalytic cultural criticism*. New York: Cornell University Press.

Branney, P. (2008). Subjectivity, not personality: Combining discourse analysis and psychoanalysis. *Social and Personality Psychology Compass*, 2, 574–590.

Brown, H. (1996). Themes in experimental research on groups from the 1930s to the 1990s. In Wetherell, M. (Ed.), *Identities, groups and social issues* (pp. 9–62). London: Sage.

Brown, R. (2000). Social identity theory: Past achievements, current problems and future challenges. *European Journal of Social Psychology*, 30(6), 745–748.

Brown, S.D., & Lunt, P. (2002). A genealogy of the social identity tradition: Deleuze and Guattari and social psychology. *British Journal of Social Psychology*, 41, 1–23.

Bruner, J.S. (1957). On perceptual readiness. *Psychological Review*, 64, 123–152.

Burman, E., & Parker, I. (1993). Introduction – discourse analysis: The turn to the text. In Burman, E., & Parker, I. (Eds.), *Discourse analytic research: Repertoires and readings of texts in action* (pp. 1–13). London: Routledge.

Chryssochoou, X. (2004). *Cultural diversity: Its social psychology*. Oxford: Blackwell Publishing.

Clark, K., & Clark, M. (1939). The development of consciousness of self and the emergence of racial identification in negro preschool children. *Journal of Social Psychology*, 10, 591–599.

Condor, S. (1996). Social identity and time. In Robinson, W.P. (Ed.), *Social groups and identities: Developing the legacy of Henri Tajfel* (pp. 285–315). Oxford: Butterworth-Heinemann.

Condor, S. (2003). 'The least doubtful promise for the future?' The short history of Tajfel's 'sociopsychological' approach to laboratory experimentation. In Laszlo, J., & Wagner, W. (Eds.), *Theories and controversies in societal psychology* (pp. 153–179). Budapest: New Mandate.

Contu, A. (2008). Decaf resistance: On misbehaviour, cynicism, and desire in liberal workplaces. *Management Communication Quarterly*, 21(3), 364–379.

Dahlstedt, M. (2004). Den massmediala förortsdjungeln: Representationer av svenska förortsmiljöer. *Nordicom Information*, 26(4), 15–29.

Daly, G. (1999). Ideology and its paradoxes: Dimensions of fantasy and enjoyment. *Journal of Political Ideologies*, 4(2), 219–238.

Dashtipour, P. (2009). *The ambivalence of resistance and identity: Using psychoanalysis in a case study of Gringo magazine.* Unpublished PhD thesis, London School of Economics and Political Science.

Dean, J. (2006). *Žižek's politics.* London: Routledge.

Dean, T. (2002). Art as symptom: Žižek and the ethics of psychoanalytic criticism. *Diacritics*, 32(2), 21–41.

Dixon J., & Durrheim K. (2000). Displacing place-identity: A discursive approach to locating self and other. *British Journal of Social Psychology*, 39, 27–44.

Dixon, J., Foster, D.H., Durrheim, K., & Wilbraham, L. (1994). Discourse and the politics of space in South Africa. *Discourse and Society*, 5, 277–296.

Dollard, J., Doob, L.W., Miller, N.E., Mowrer, O.H., & Sears, R.R. (1939). *Frustration and aggression.* New Haven, CT: Yale University Press.

Duncan, G.A. (2001). Black youth, ethics, and the politics of respectability in psychological research. *International Journal of Critical Psychology*, 15, 85–103.

Duveen, G. (2001). Representations, identities and resistance. In Deaux, K., & Philogene, G. (Eds.), *Representations of the social* (pp. 257–270). Oxford: Blackwell.

Eagleton, T. (1991). *Ideology: An introduction.* London: Verso.

Edwards, D. (1998). The relevant thing about her: Social identity categories in use. In Antaki, C., & Widdicombe, S. (Eds.), *Identities in talk* (pp. 15–33). London: Sage.

Fairclough, N. (1989). *Language and power.* London: Longman.

Fairclough, N. (1992). Intertextuality in critical discourse analysis. *Linguistics and Education*, 4, 269–293.

Fanon, F. (1990). *The wretched of the earth.* London: Penguin.

Farr, R. (1996). *The roots of modern social psychology, 1872–1954.* Cambridge, MA: Blackwell.

Festinger, L. (1954). A theory of social comparison processes. *Human Relations*, 7, 117–140.

Fink, B. (1999). *A clinical introduction to Lacanian psychoanalysis: Theory and technique.* London: Harvard University Press.

Fink, B. (2003). The subject and the Other's desire. In Žižek, S. (Ed.), *Jacques Lacan: Critical evaluations in cultural theory* (pp. 243–263). London: Routledge.

Freud, S. (1927). Fetishism. In Strachey, J. (Ed.), *Standard edition of the complete psychological works of Sigmund Freud.* (Vol. 21, pp. 149–157). London: Hogarth Press and the Institute of Psychoanalysis.

Freud, S. (1955). Totem and taboo: Resemblances between the mental lives of savages and neurotics. In Strachey, J. (Ed.), *Standard edition of the complete works of Sigmund Freud.* (Vol. 13, pp. 1–164). London: Hogarth Press and the Institute of Psychoanalysis.

Freud, S. (1957). Mourning and melancholia. In Strachey, J. (Ed.), *Standard edition of the complete works of Sigmund Freud.* (Vol. 14, pp. 243–260). London: Hogarth Press and the Institute of Psychoanalysis.

Freud, S. (1959). *Group psychology and the analysis of the ego.* New York: Norton.

Frosh, S. (1999). What is outside discourse? *Psychoanalytic Studies*, 1(4), 381–390.

Frosh, S. (2002). Enjoyment, bigotry, discourse and cognition. *British Journal of Social Psychology*, 41, 189–193.

Frosh, S. (2003). *Key concepts in psychoanalysis*. New York: New York University Press.

Frosh, S. (2008). On negative critique: A reply. *Psychoanalysis, Culture and Society*, 13, 416–422.

Frosh, S., Phoenix, A., & Pattman, R. (2003). Taking a stand: Using psychoanalysis to explore the positioning of subjects in discourse. *British Journal of Social Psychology*, 42, 39–53.

Georgaca, E. (2005). Lacanian psychoanalysis and the subject of social constructionist psychology: Analysing subjectivity in talk. *International Journal of Critical Psychology*, 14, 74–94.

Gerard, H.B., & Hoyt, M.F. (1974). Distinctiveness of social categorization and attitude towards ingroup members. *Journal of Personality and Social Psychology*, 29, 836–842.

Gill, R. (1996). Discourse analysis: Practical implementation. In Richardson, J.T.E. (Ed.), *Handbook of qualitative research methods for psychology and the social sciences* (pp. 141–156). Leicester: BPS Books.

Glynos, J. (2001). The grip of ideology: A Lacanian approach to the theory of ideology. *Journal of Political Ideologies*, 6(2), 191–214.

Glynos, J. (2003). Self-transgression and freedom. *Critical Review of International Social and Political Philosophy*, 6(2), 1–20.

Glynos, J., & Stavrakakis, Y. (2003). Encounters of the real kind. *Journal of Lacanian Studies*, 1(1), 110–128.

Glynos, J., & Stavrakakis, Y. (2008). Lacan and political subjectivity: Fantasy and enjoyment in psychoanalysis and political theory. *Subjectivity*, 24, 256–274.

Gough, B. (2004). Psychoanalysis as a resource for understanding emotional ruptures in the text: The case of defensive masculinities. *British Journal of Social Psychology*, 43, 245–267.

Hall, S. (1991). Old and new identities, old and new ethnicities. In King, A.D. (Ed.), *Culture, globalisation and the world system: Contemporary positions for the representation of identity* (pp. 31–68). London: Macmillan.

Hall, S. (1996). Who needs identity? In Hall, S., & Du Gay, P. (Eds.), *Questions of cultural identity* (pp. 1–17). London: Sage.

Hall, S. (1997). The spectacle of the "Other". In Hall, S. (Ed.), *Representation: Cultural representations and signifying practices* (pp. 223–290). London: Sage.

Harstone, M., & Augoustinos, M. (1995). The minimal group paradigm: Categorization into two versus three groups. *European Journal of Social Psychology*, 25(2), 179–193.

Henriques, J. (1984). Social psychology and the politics of racism. In Henrique, J., Hollway, W., Urwin, C., Venn, C., & Walkerdine, V. (Eds.), *Changing the subject: Psychology, social regulation, and subjectivity* (pp. 60–90). London: Routledge.

Henriques, J., Hollway, W., Urwin, C., Venn, C., & Walkerdine, V. (1984). *Changing the subject: Psychology, social regulation, and subjectivity*. London: Routledge.

Hertel, G., & Kerr, N.L. (2001). Priming in-group favoritism: The impact of normative scripts in the minimal group paradigm. *Journal of Experimental Social Psychology*, 37, 316–324.

Hinkle, S., & Brown, R.J. (1990). Intergroup comparisons and social identity: Some links and lacunae. In Abrams, D., & Hogg, M.A. (Eds.), *Social identity theory: Constructive and critical advances* (pp. 48–70). Hemel Hempstead: Harvester Wheatsheaf.

Hogg, M.A. (2000). Subjective uncertainty reduction through self-categorisation: A motivational theory of social identity processes. *European Review of Social Psychology*, 11, 223–255.

Hogg, M.A. (2001). A social identity theory of leadership. *Personality and Social Psychology Review*, 5(3), 184–200.

Hogg, M.A., & Abrams, D. (1988). *Social identifications: A social psychology of intergroup relations and group processes*. London: Routledge.

Hogg, M.A., & Abrams, D. (1993). Towards a single-process uncertainty-reduction model of social motivation in groups. In Hogg, M.A., & Abrams, D. (Eds.), *Group motivation: Social psychological perspectives* (pp. 173–190). Hemel Hempstead: Harvester Wheatsheaf.

Hogg, M.A., & Hardie, E.A. (1991). Social attraction, personal attraction, and self-categorisation: A field study. *Personality and Social Psychology Bulletin*, 17, 175–1980.

Hogg, M.A., & McGarty, C. (1990). Self-categorisation and social identity. In Abrams, D., & Hogg, M.A. (Eds.), *Social identity theory: Constructive and critical advances* (pp. 10–27). Hemel Hempstead: Harvester Wheatsheaf.

Hollway, W., & Jefferson, T. (2000). *Doing qualitative research differently: Free association, narrative and the interview method*. London: Sage.

Hook, D. (2005). Affecting whiteness: Racism as technology of affect. *International Journal of Critical Psychology*, 16, 74–99.

Hook, D. (2006). "Pre-discursive" racism. *Journal of Community and Applied Social Psychology*, 16, 207–232.

Hook, D. (2007). *Foucault, psychology and the analytics of power*. Houndmills, Hampshire: Palgrave Macmillan.

Hook, D. (2008a). Absolute Other: Lacan's 'big Other' as adjunct to critical social psychological analysis. *Social and Personality Psychology Compass*, 2(1), 51–73.

Hook, D. (2008b). Articulating psychoanalytic and psychosocial studies: Limitations and possibilities. *Psychoanalysis, Culture and Society*, 30, 397–405.

Hopkins, N., & Kahani-Hopkins, V. (2004). Identity construction and British Muslims' political activity: Beyond rational actor theory. *British Journal of Social Psychology*, 43, 339–356.

Hopkins, N., Kahani-Hopkins, V., & Reicher, S. (2006). Identity and social change: Contextualizing agency. *Feminism and Psychology*, 16, 52–57.

Hopkins, N., Reicher, S., & Kahani-Hopkins, V. (2003). Citizenship, participation and identity construction: Political mobilization amongst British Muslims. *Psychologica Belgica*, 43, 33–54.

Hornsey, M.J. (2008). Social identity theory and self-categorisation theory: A historical review. *Social and Personality Psychology Compass*, 2, 204–222.

Howarth, C. (2002). Identity in whose eyes? The role of representations in identity construction. *Journal of the Theory of Social Behaviour*, 32, 145–162.

Huddy, L. (2001). From social to political identity: A critical examination of social identity theory. *Political Psychology*, 22, 127–155.

Hylton, P.L., & Miller, H. (2004). Now that we've found love what are we gonna do with it? A narrative understanding of Black identity. *Theory and Psychology*, 14, 373–408.

Kirkwood, S., Liu, J.H., & Weatherall, A. (2005). Challenging the standard story of indigenous rights in Aotearoa/New Zealand. *Journal of Community and Applied Social Psychology*, 15, 493–505.

Lacan, J. (1977). *Ecrit: A selection*. London: Tavistock/Routledge.

Lacatus, C. (2007). What is a *blatte*? Migration and ethnic identity in contemporary Sweden. *Journal of Arab and Muslim Media Research*, 1(1), 79–92.

Le Bon, G. (1896). *The crowd: A study of the popular mind*. London: T.F. Unwin.

Lynn, N., & Lea, S. (2003). 'A phantom menace and the new apartheid': The social construction of asylum-seekers in the United Kingdom. *Discourse & Society*, 14, 425–452.

Marchak, C. (1990). The joy of transgression: Bataille and Kristeva. *Philosophy Today*, 34(4), 354–363.

Milani, T.M. (2010). What's in a name? Language ideology and social differentiation in a Swedish print-mediated debate. *Journal of Sociolinguistics*, 14(1), 116–142.

Moscovici, S., & Paicheler, G. (1978). Social comparison and social recognition: Two complementary processes of identification. In Tajfel, H. (Ed.), *Differentiation between social groups* (pp. 261–266). London: Academic.

Mulinari, D., & Neergaard, A. (2005). "Black Skull" consciousness: The new Swedish working class. *Race and Class*, 46(3), 55–72.

Oakes, P. (1987). The salience of social categories. In Turner, J.C., Hogg, M., Oakes, P., Reicher, S., & Wetherell, M. (Eds.), *Rediscovering the social group: A self-categorisation theory* (pp. 117–141). Oxford: Blackwell.

Oakes, P.J., Haslam, S.A., & Turner, J.C. (1994). *Stereotyping, and social reality*. Oxford: Blackwell.

Parker, I. (1989). Discourse and power. In Shotter, J., & Gergen, K.J. (Eds.), *Texts of identity* (pp. 57–69). London: Sage.

Parker, I. (1992). *Discourse dynamics: Critical analysis for social and individual psychology*. London and New York: Routledge.

Parker, I. (1997). Group identity and individuality in times of crisis: Psychoanalytic reflections on social psychological knowledge. *Human Relations*, 50, 183–196.

Parker, I. (2000). Looking for Lacan: Virtual psychology. In Malone, K., & Friedlander, S. (Eds.), *The subject of Lacan: A Lacanian Reader for psychologists*. New York: SUNY Press.

Parker, I. (2003). Jacques Lacan, barred psychologist. *Theory and Psychology*, 13(1), 95–115.

Parker, I. (2005). *Qualitative psychology: Introducing radical research*. Maidenhead: Open University Press.

Parker, I. (2007). *Revolution in psychology: Alienation to emancipation*. London: Pluto Press.

Pavón Cuéllar, D. (2010). *From the conscious interior to an exterior unconscious: Lacan, discourse analysis and social psychology.* London: Karnac Books.

Potter, J., & Wetherell, M. (1987). *Discourse and social psychology: Beyond attitudes and behaviour.* London: Sage.

Reicher, S. (1996). Social identity and social change: Rethinking the context of social psychology. In Robinson, W.P. (Ed.), *Social groups and identities: Developing the legacy of Henri Tajfel* (pp. 317–336). Oxford: Butterworth-Heinemann.

Reicher, S. (2004). The context of social identity: Domination, resistance and change. *Political Psychology*, 25, 921–945.

Reicher, S., & Hopkins, N. (1996). Self-category constructions in political rhetoric: An analysis of Thatcher's and Kinnock's speeches concerning the British miners' strike (1984–5). *European Journal of Social Psychology*, 26, 353–371.

Reicher, S., & Hopkins, N. (2001a). Psychology and the end of history: A critique and a proposal for the psychology of social categorization. *International Society of Political Psychology*, 22(2), 383–407.

Reicher, S., & Hopkins, N. (2001b). *Self and nation.* London: Sage.

Reicher, S., Spears, R., & Haslam, S.A. (2010). The social identity approach in social psychology. In Wetherell, M., & Talpade-Mohanty, C. (Eds.), *The Sage handbook of identities* (pp. 45–62). London: Sage.

Rose, J. (1996). *States of fantasy.* Oxford: Clarendon.

Rosenthal, R. (1966). *Experimenter effects in behavioural research.* New York: Appleton.

Saussure, F. de (1974). *Course in general linguistics.* Glasgow: Fontana/Collins.

Schori, M. (2008). Förundersökningen mot Gringo-gänget läggs ner. *Dagens media*, 17 June. Available at: http://www.dagensmedia.se/mallar/dagensmedia_mall.asp? version=173348 (Accessed June 2007).

Sherif, M., Harvey, O.J., White, B.J., Hood, W.R., & Sherif, C.W. (1961). *Intergroup conflict and cooperation: The Robbers Cave experiment.* Norman, OK: Institute of Group Relations.

Stavrakakis, Y. (2007). *The Lacanian left: Psychoanalysis, theory, politics.* Edinburgh: Edinburgh University Press.

Stavrakakis, Y. (2008). Peripheral vision: Subjectivity and the organised Other: Between symbolic authority and fantasmatic enjoyment. *Organisation Studies*, 29(7), 1037–1059.

St Claire, L., & Turner, J.C. (1982). The role of demand characteristics in the social categorization paradigm. *European Journal of Social Psychology*, 13(3), 307–314.

Tajfel, H. (1970). Experiments in intergroup discrimination. *Scientific American*, 233, 96–102.

Tajfel, H. (1974). Social identity and intergroup behaviour. *Social Science Information*, 13, 65–93.

Tajfel, H. (1978). Social categorisation, social identity and social comparison. In Tajfel, H. (Ed.), *Differentiation between social groups: Studies in the social psychology of intergroup relations* (pp. 61–76). London: Academic.

Tajfel, H. (1981). *Human groups and social categories.* Cambridge: Cambridge University Press.

Tajfel, H. (1982). *Social identity and intergroup relations*. Cambridge: Cambridge University Press.

Tajfel, H., Billig, M., Bundy, R.P., & Flament, C. (1971). Social categorization and intergroup behaviour. *European Journal of Social Psychology*, 1, 149–177.

Tajfel, H., & Turner, J.C. (1986). The social identity theory of intergroup behaviour. In Worchel, S., & Austin, L.W. (Eds.), *Psychology of intergroup relations* (pp. 7–24). Chicago: Nelson-Hall.

Tajfel, H., & Wilkes, A.L. (1963). Classification and quantitative judgment. *British Journal of Psychology*. 54, 101–114.

Turner, J.C. (1981). The experimental social psychology of intergroup behaviour. In Turner, J.C., & Giles, H. (Eds.), *Intergroup behaviour* (pp. 66–101). Oxford: Basil Blackwell.

Turner, J.C. (1985). Social categorisation and the self-concept: A social cognitive theory of group behaviour. In Lawler, E.J. (Ed.), *Advances in group processes* (pp. 77–102). Greenwich, CT: Jai Press.

Turner, J.C. (1987). Preface. In Turner, J.C., Hogg, M., Oakes, P., Reicher, S., & Wetherell, M. (Eds.), *Rediscovering the social group: A self-categorisation theory* (pp. vii–x). Oxford: Basil Blackwell.

Turner, J.C. (1991). *Social influence*. Milton Keynes: Open University Press.

Turner, J.C. (1996). Henri Tajfel: An introduction. In Robinson, W.P (Ed.), *Social groups and identities: Developing the legacy of Henri Tajfel* (pp. 1–23). Oxford: Butterworth-Heinemann.

Turner, J.C. (1999). Some current issues in research on social identity and self-categorization theories. In Ellemers, N., Spears, R., & Doosje, B. (Eds.), *Social identity: Context, commitment, content* (pp. 6–34). Oxford: Blackwell.

Turner, J.C. (2005). Explaining the nature of power: A three-process theory. *European Journal of Social Psychology*, 35, 1–22.

Turner, J.C., & Brown, R.J. (1978). Social status, cognitive alternatives and intergroup relations. In Tajfel, H. (Ed.), *Differentiation between social groups* (pp. 201–234). London: Academic.

Turner, J.C., & Giles, H. (Eds.) (1981). *Intergroup behaviour*. Oxford: Blackwell.

Turner, J.C., Hogg, M., Oakes, P., Reicher, S., & Wetherell, M. (1987). *Rediscovering the social group: A self-categorisation theory*. Oxford: Basil Blackwell.

Vanheule, S., & Verhaeghe, P. (2009). Identity through a psychoanalytic looking glass. *Theory and Psychology*, 19, 391–411.

Verkuyten, M. (2005). *The social psychology of ethnic identity*. Hove: Psychology Press.

Walkerdine, V. (2006). Workers in the new economy: Transformation as border crossing. *Ethos*, 34(1), 10–41.

Wetherell, M. (1982). Cross-cultural studies of minimal groups: Implications for the social identity theory of intergroup relations. In Tajfel, H. (Ed.), *Social identity and intergroup relations* (pp. 207–240). Cambridge: Cambridge University Press.

Wetherell, M. (1996a). Constructing social identities: The individual/social binary in Henri Tajfel's social psychology. In Robinson, W.P. (Ed.), *Social groups and identities: Developing the legacy of Henri Tajfel* (pp. 269–284). Oxford: Butterworth-Heinemann.

Wetherell, M. (1996b). Group conflict and the social psychology of racism. In Wetherell, M.S. (Ed.), *Identities, groups and social issues* (pp. 175–238). London: Sage.

Wetherell, M. (1996c). Introduction. In Wetherell, M. (Ed.), *Identities, groups and social issues* (pp. 1–8). London: Sage.

Wetherell, M. (1996d). Life histories/social histories. In Wetherell, M. (Ed.), *Identities, groups and social issues* (pp. 299–361). London: Sage.

Wetherell, M. (2004). Themes in discourse research: The case of Diana. In Wetherell, M., Taylor, S., & Yates, S.J. (Eds.), *Discourse theory and practice* (pp. 14–28). London: Sage.

Wetherell, M., & Potter, J. (1992). *Mapping the language of racism: Discourse and the legitimation of exploitation.* Hemel Hempstead: Harvester Wheatsheaf.

Witt-Brattström, E. (2006a). Miljonsvenskan – en mediebluff. *Dagens Nyheter*, [internet] 13 May. Available at: http://www.dn.se/kultur-noje/miljonsvenskan-en-mediebluff-1.695563 (Accessed July 2006).

Witt-Brattström, E. (2006b). Vem äger svenskan? *Dagens Nyheter*, [internet] 19 April. Available at: http://www.dn.se/kultur-noje/vem-ager-svenskan-1.643868 (Accessed July 2006).

Žižek, S. (1989). *The sublime object of ideology.* London: Verso.

Žižek, S. (1993). *Tarrying with the negative.* Durham, NC: Duke University Press.

Žižek, S. (1997). *The plague of fantasies.* London: Verso.

Žižek, S. (2006). *How to read Lacan.* London: Granta.

Žižek, S. (2008). *Violence: Six sideways reflections.* London: Profile Books.

Index

Note: The letter 'n' following the locators denotes the note number in the text